# Public Services in India

## *Current Good Practices and New Developments in Public Service Management*

COMMONWEALTH SECRETARIAT

RAWAT PUBLICATIONS

Jaipur • New Delhi • Bangalore • Mumbai • Hyderabad • Guwahati

ISBN 81-316-0139-0

**Indian Reprint, 2007**



This work, originally issued as *A Profile of the Public Service of India*, is published by arrangement with the Commonwealth Secretariat.



*Published by*
Prem Rawat for **Rawat Publications**
Satyam Apts., Sector 3, Jawahar Nagar, Jaipur - 302 004 (India)
Phone: 0141 265 1748 / 7006 Fax: 0141 265 1748
E-mail : info@rawatbooks.com
Website: rawatbooks.com

*New Delhi Office*
4858/24, Ansari Road, Daryaganj, New Delhi 110 002
Phone: 011-23263290

*Also at Bangalore, Mumbai, Hyderabad and Guwahati*

Printed at Chaman Enterprises, New Delhi.

## Acknowledgements

The Commonwealth Secretariat gratefully acknowledges the Ministry of Personnel, Public Grievances and Pensions (Department of Administrative Reforms and Public Grievances), Government of India, in the preparation of this profile of the Public Service of India entitled *Current Good Practices and New Developments in Public Service Management*.

The Secretariat places on record its sincere thanks to CAPAM for its co-ordination and its appreciation to Dr P. S. A. Sundaram for having accepted the challenge of writing this paper and having completed the job with a high degree of commitment and excellence.

# Contents

# Abbreviations

| | |
|---|---|
| ACC | Appointments Committee of the Cabinet |
| ACP | Assured Career Progression |
| ACR | Annual Confidential Roll |
| AIS | All India Services |
| ARC | Administrative Reforms Commission |
| ASCI | Administrative Staff College of India |
| ARPG | Administrative Reforms and Public Grievances |
| ATI | Administrative Training Institute (in states) |
| CAPAM | Commonwealth Association for Public Administration and Management |
| CARD | Computer-aided Registration of Documents |
| CAT | Central Administrative Tribunal |
| C&AG | Comptroller and Auditor General of India |
| CBI | Central Bureau of Investigation |
| CDI | Commissioners for Departmental Inquiries |
| CGG | Centre for Good Governance (Andhra Pradesh) |
| COBRA | Committee of Bangalore Residents Associations |
| COPE | Commission on People's Empowerment |
| CSMOP | Central Secretariat Manual of Office Procedure |
| CSS | Central Secretariat Service |
| CVC | Central Vigilance Commissioner |
| DIT | Department of Information Technology |
| DMP | Disaster Management Plan |
| DOPT | Department of Personnel and Training |
| DPC | Departmental Promotion Committee |
| DTS | Design of Training Skills |
| ERC | Expenditure Reforms Commission (2001) |
| FCPC | Fifth Central Pay Commission (1996) |
| HPC | High Powered Committee |
| IAS | Indian Administrative Service |
| ICT | Information and Communication Technology |
| IFOS | Indian Forest Service |
| IIM | Indian Institute of Management |
| IAMR | Institute for Applied Manpower Research |
| IPS | Indian Police Service |
| ISTM | Institute of Secretariat Training and Management |
| JCM | Joint Consultative Machinery |

| | |
|---|---|
| JFM | Joint Forest Management |
| LAN | Local Area Network |
| LBSNAA | Lal Bahadur Shastri National Academy of Administration |
| MKSS | Mazdur Kisan Sangharsh Samiti (Association for Struggle of Farmers and Workers) |
| MSOP | Manual of Secretariat Office Procedure |
| MTEF | Medium Term Expenditure Framework |
| O&M | Organisation and Management |
| OBC | Other Backward Classes |
| OSNSS | One-stop, non-stop shops |
| PAC | Public Affairs Centre (Bangalore) |
| PESB | Public Enterprises Selection Board |
| PIM | Participatory Irrigation Management |
| PPGP | Personnel, Public Grievances and Pensions |
| PRI | Panchayati Raj Institutions (rural elected bodies) |
| PSC | Public Service Commission |
| RTO | Regional Transport Office |
| SAARC | South Asian Association for Regional Co-operation |
| SC | Scheduled Classes |
| SHGs | Self-help Groups |
| SSC | Staff Selection Commission |
| SIU | Staff Inspection Unit |
| SMART | Simple, Moral, Accountable, Responsive and Transparent |
| ST | Scheduled Tribes |
| TOT | Training of Trainers |
| TQM | Total Quality Management |
| TNVPN | Tamil Nadu Virtual Private Network |
| ULB | Urban Local Body |
| UPSC | Union Public Service Commission |
| WAN | Wide Area Network |
| YASHADA | Yashwantrao Chavan Academy of Development Administration, Pune |

## Foreword to the Country Profiles series

Since the successful launch of the Commonwealth Profiles series in 1995, much has happened. When the Auckland CHOGM of 1995 mandated its 'Towards a New Public Administration' Programme, many Commonwealth member countries, to a greater or lesser degree, were contemplating or already applying the principles of the New Public Management (NPM) in their civil services. Since that time, the literature on the NPM has been burgeoning, the architecture of civil service delivery has altered dramatically and the debate about the relative success or failure of the NPM continues. In practical terms, the civil services described in the *Profile* series back in 1995 are now often radically different from the scope, organisation and approach of the same civil services today.

The Governance and Institutional Development Division (GIDD) has decided that it is timely to revise and re-issue an updated Profiles Series which attempts both to describe and explain the often tumultuous and controversial public sector reforms of the last seven years as they have unfolded in the contributing countries.

We want these updated Profiles to continue to be a readable, accessible and valuable series, especially for practising civil servants, and to serve as reference points for diplomatic, bilateral, multilateral, political and academic audiences.

**Dr Victor Ayeni**
*Director,*
*Governance and Institutional Development Division*

**Dr Peter Frost**
*Special Adviser,*
*Public Sector Reform,*
*Governance and Institutional Development Division*

# 1 Overview

## From Controls to Liberalisation

The present context of Indian public administration can be understood only in terms of changing policies for economic planning and the responsibilities assumed by the administration. When the country set out in 1950s on the road to a socialistic pattern of society and central planning, government direct intervention manifested itself in the regulation and licensing of economic and social activity and the establishment of a huge public sector in all aspects of the economy. The most rapid expansion of functions and public services occurred in the first four decades after independence, but the size of many ministries and state governments continued to increase up to the end of the twentieth century.

Starting in 1991, the central government initiated a wide-ranging programme of economic reform, liberalisation and structural adjustment. Economic reform is part of the political idiom among all major political parties with some critical differences of view on the pace and sequence of reduced state control and privatisation of state enterprises. The public sector is much less dominant than it used to be in many critical sectors and its relative position is likely to decline further as government ownership in many existing public sector organisations is reduced. There has been uncertain progress in the rationalisation of functions and portfolios. However, the recent constitutional amendment to limit the size of central and state ministries augurs well for a fresh initiative in this direction.

## Centre-state relations and the Critical Role of States

The Indian Constitution has a federal character with a distinct unitary bias. The Constitution provides for multi-level governance, with both the central and state governments having their own executive, legislature and judiciary and exercising powers according to a division and lists mandated in the Constitution. At the same time, most areas of governance of critical importance for citizens, such as law and order, city and district government, education and health, are the responsibility of state and local government.

A variety of factors accentuate the dependence of the states on central government under the present constitutional framework: the dominance of a single political party in central and state governments in the first three decades of independence; centralised economic planning; control by central government over the location of enterprises and the channelling of public investment; and the power to impose a state of emergency.

The institutions of All India Services (AIS) and the Comptroller and Auditor General (C&AG) mean that there is an integrated administration and audit system. Thanks to the legacy of uniform administration and civil service practices, it is much easier to replicate good practices in central ministries and across states. This has been leveraged by the instruments of central financial assistance.

Various factors have made the quality of states' own economic and social management and public administration an important determinant of growth and pro-poor performance. There is increasing stress on the concept of co-operative federalism, based on mutual trust and reaching decisions by consensus. Subject to broad national priorities, the states have the freedom to determine not only their own priorities but also the modalities of public intervention and the provision of goods and services.

## Democratic Decentralisation and Citizen Movements

Federalism has been taken to a decentralised level following the 73rd and 74th constitutional amendments, which elevated the status of elected local bodies and set up district planning committees to sustain people's participation. The amendments were followed by laws in the states setting up a third tier of government with specific functions and installing *Panchayati Raj* Institutions (PRI) in rural areas and *Nagarpalikas,* or municipal councils, in urban areas.

Democratic decentralisation has been paralleled by the burgeoning movement for community and user management of natural resources and services at the local level and citizen oversight of local administration. State support for civil society efforts is symbolised by watershed and forest management committees, village education and health committees in rural areas, and neighbourhood committees and sanitation committees of citizens, including poor and vulnerable groups in cities.

## Recent Milestones in Administrative Reform: the FCPC and ERC

Significant milestones in civil service reform in the last five years have been the report of the Fifth Central Pay Commission (FCPC, 1997), the report of the Expenditure Reforms Commission (ERC, 2001), the National Human Development Report (2001), the report of the National Commission to review the Constitution (2003), the tenth Five-year Plan (2002–2007) and the report of the Surendranath Committee on Performance Appraisal (2003).

Both the FCPC and the ERC made far-reaching suggestions for optimising the workforce and restructuring government. They advocated that civil service reform should deal with issues of size, productivity, accountability and integrity of the public services. The FCPC pointed out the problems arising from lack of autonomy and flexibility, rigid procedures, fragmented cadres, political interference and the absence of a credible regime of incentives and sanctions for performance. It enunciated an efficiency programme setting how to redefine the goals of government, contract out certain non-core activities and change work methods.

The FCPC made its generous proposals for enhanced pay and allowances conditional on the adoption of a strategy for optimising the workforce. Unfortunately, government did not follow through quickly on the conditions attaching to the award and the states followed the example of the centre. The Expenditure Reforms Commission (2001) drew attention to the growing cost of government employment and pensions in the centre and states following the liberal awards to employees. It carried forward the suggestions of the FCPC in terms of institutionalised measures for downsizing the workforce, such as a voluntary retirement scheme, attrition and department level recruitment plans. The Commission's identification of surplus staff was linked to scientific functional reviews, scope for automation and privatisation and reduction of the large complement of support staff. Government has implemented many of these suggestions.

National policies on health, education and social services have reflected the concern for responsive delivery and consultation. This is matched by efforts to integrate all sector programmes and poverty alleviation schemes at a decentralised level through local bodies and district administration.

## The Role of the State

In the course of the rationalisation of functions, it has been realised that what is involved is not so much a drastic reduction as a reordering and reorientation of the role of the state. There is general agreement that there is a continuing rationale for the government to increase its involvement in poverty reduction and basic infrastructure, in environmental protection, maintaining law and order, effective dispute resolution, swift access to justice and in the protection and empowerment of the weaker sections of the community. Elections are increasingly fought on the governance platform at the national and state level.

The location of the second-generation reforms following the first wave of liberalisation is as much in the centre as in the states. The reforms are driven as much by fiscal crisis as by the political movement for good governance. It is increasingly realised by governments and aid agencies alike that policies for fiscal sustainability and governance improvements are inter-linked. Progress is spurred by virtuous competition among states and by fiscal leverage from the central government.

## Good Governance

The central government organised a conference of state chief ministers in May 1997 to consider an action plan for effective and responsive administration. The action plan of this conference and the reports of the FCPC and the ERC set the tone for administrative reform and sharing of experience in state governments as well. Some of them set up, commissions to consider administrative reforms and task forces on good governance.

Government is proceeding on the basis of a five-point programme of good governance advanced by the Prime Minister before the chief ministers in 2003:

- A comprehensive legal framework, that is defended and enforced by an impartial and competent judicial system;
- A framework that is accountable and open;
- A transparent executive decision-making apparatus;
- A system coupled with a capable, efficient and people-friendly bureaucracy, and a strong civil society.

The Action Plan on Good Governance, prepared by the Inter State Council in 2003, will now be elaborated by a sub-committee under the Deputy Prime Minister. A core group under the Cabinet Secretary has approved an Implementation Matrix containing 29 action points with reference to customer orientation, delegation, outsourcing and improved administrative practices. In March 2004 government set up an expert committee under the chairmanship of the former Chairman of the Union Public Service Commission (UPSC) to advise on specific steps to advance the Action Plan.

Once a national policy for information technology and communication had been put in place in 1998, the idea of electronic governance began to gain ground. Electronic governance has been seen by political leaders and bureaucrats alike as a synonym for an IT-driven system of governance that works better, costs less, empowers citizens and is capable of responding to citizens' needs for quick and quality services.

## Prospects in States

In reflecting upon the varying improvements in the quality of governance and public management in different Indian states, some important causative factors emerge.

- The tremendous influence that the state's electoral composition, continuity of political leadership and instability of regimes can exert on the government's ability to pursue a ongoing reform agenda;
- The role of champions for reform of committed technocrats at the top and middle levels of the administration and in training

institutions, and the need to provide avenues of support for nurturing this championship;

- The extent of government receptivity to offers of assistance from civil society and the scope for vast improvements in administration through partnerships;
- The importance of documenting, replicating and scaling up the islands of success in different central ministries and states; and
- The inter-linked nature of reforms in different areas, such as the criticality of stable tenures for service delivery or deregulation and transparency for preventing corruption.

These five factors raise important issues related to the institutionalisation of reform and the need to ensure that reforms do not fade away with the personalities who introduced them.

## A Scorecard

At the risk of oversimplification, the following table presents a SWOT analysis of the Indian public service.

**The Indian Public Service – A SWOT Analysis**

| Strengths | Opportunities |
|---|---|
| • Mature and consolidated democracy<br>• Co-operative federalism and spirit of accommodation among states and Centre<br>• Stability of central and state governments<br>• Highly capable senior executive service, backed by constitutional protection<br>• Commitment to greater devolution of functions and resources to elected local bodies and emergence of local leadership<br>• Growing strength of civil society, user management of services and citizen led initiatives | • Commitment of national leadership and senior bureaucracy to reform<br>• Consensus across political parties on economic reform and action plan for good governance<br>• Efforts to rein in salary and pension costs<br>• Experimentation with innovative organisational forms and re-engineering at sector and local level<br>• Growing national confidence and citizen demand for improved administration<br>• Virtuous competition among states for citizen-centred administration, transparency and electronic governance |

**Strengths** (contin.)

- Active judiciary in support of citizen rights and protection from maladministration
- Network of institutions of higher learning and highly skilled IT and communication industry and workforce
- Strong presence in global deliberations on trade and commerce
- Open society with burgeoning middle class

**Weaknesses**

- Vast country with varying resource endowments, political commitments and administrative capacities across regions
- Low levels of per capita income, acute inequality and poverty
- Persisting problems of access to education and health care, especially for poor and socially disadvantaged groups
- Centralised, fragmented and hierarchical systems of administration, weak mechanisms for co-ordination and unwillingness to delegate authority
- Unaffordable increase in salary and pension costs
- Rigid and cumbersome regulations that affect citizens and employees alike
- Absence of credible, open and participatory systems for performance assessment
- Absence of credible regime for incentives and sanctions and failure to promptly weed out inefficient and dishonest employees

**Opportunities** (contin.)

- Legal and regulatory reform
- Constructive dialogue between government, private business and civil society on governance issues
- Citizen oversight of transparency, administrative performance and integrity
- Growing body of local innovators, good governance practices, public-private partnerships and user management of services and the interest of government and people in scaling up the practices
- Explosion in communication and ideas, fuelled by a free media and use of IT and globalisation

**Threats**

- Risk of declining political commitment to rationalisation of functions, civil service reform, transparency and decentralisation
- Politicisation of civil service and unstable tenures of officials
- Inability to cope with trade union pressures for more benefits and allowances
- Opposition to rightsizing civil service and public sector reform from vested interests
- Frustration of employees over lack of incentives for improved performance or prompt punishment of inefficient behaviour
- Continuing perception of corruption and unresponsiveness in administration
- Resistance from vested interests to reform
- Large numbers of untrained and less skilled staff at lower levels

# 2 Structure and Evolution of the Indian Public Service

## 2.1 Structure of the Federal and State Governments

India gained independence in August 1947. The Indian Federation is composed of 28 states and seven union territories in a country of sub-continental proportions with a population of little over a billion in 2001. The Constitution has installed a parliamentary democracy on the Westminster model. It is important to appreciate the fact that political entities, with differing historical backgrounds and administrative traditions were constitutionally grouped into states through the historic process before and following independence in 1947.

As do other federal constitutions, the Indian Constitution provides for a division of functions and financial resources between the central and state governments and lays down the mechanism for the devolution of federal resources to states. (The terms 'central' and 'Union' government are also used to designate the federal government in India.) The Constitution has devolved 66 subject areas to the states, apart from ability to legislate on subjects in the concurrent list. Both the regulatory and developmental administration fall in the sphere of the state, including areas such as police, law and order, agriculture, education, housing and basic services, industries, health, forests and fisheries. There is a concurrent list which contains areas such as economic and social planning and labour, where policies are jointly framed and implemented by the central and state governments.

India has over 4,368 towns, 35 metropolitan cities and nearly 600,000 villages, all of which fall under the state governments. The basic territorial units of state administration in India are the districts into which each state is sub-divided. For the purpose of revenue administration (which predates local self-government in India), the district is further split into subdivisions, *tehsils* (smaller blocks) and circles. The districts (numbering about 530) are composed into sub-districts called *tehsils* or *mandals* depending on the state. The district forms the basis of panchayati raj or local government institutions as well, starting with the *zilla parishad* (district council) at the district level. However, the formation of the tiers of block and village panchayat (elected council) varies according to local needs.

The district is the unit of administration for the police and various regulatory and development departments, and has also been the operating unit for various central and state schemes under the Five Year Plans ever since the launch of the original plan. The Collector, or District Magistrate, represents the state government in its totality, in the manner of the French Prefect. With an urban population about the size of the population of the USA, effective urban management is a crucial element of public administration.

## 2.2 Structure and Character of the Public Service

The Indian Constitution provides for central and state public service commissions, the All India Services and administrative tribunals. It assures security and protection from arbitrary punishment, and dismissal and removal from service or reduction in rank after reasonable opportunity and due process. While the central government is supported by various organised and isolated services, the state governments operate with their own services for administration at state and local levels, subject to the unifying role of the All India Services.

The high capacity of India's civil service is derived from constitutional protection, meritocratic recruitment, the high level of competition in civil service examinations (under 1 per cent of applicants qualified in recent years for the higher services) and a mix of technically and non-technically educated entrants. Technical capability and occupational demands are reasonably matched within the three All-India Services and the functionally specialised central and state services given the existing training facilities.

Public servants derive their powers and authority from the Constitution and various Acts and rules which give legal sanction. The exercise of this authority is subject to scrutiny by a number of institutions such as the courts of law and tribunals and the

Comptroller and Auditor General of India. The legislature is, of course, competent to debate any executive action and give directions through resolutions and committee reports. The media has increasingly played a watchdog role in exposing waste, inefficiency and violations of the law.

### *Box 2.1* Features of the Indian Civil Service

**The important features of the Civil Service, which also affect the quality of administration, include:**

- **Uniform personnel management practices and secretariat procedures in all departments;**
- **Distinction between policy and administration;**
- **The tenure system of staffing and the compulsory periodic transfer of staff;**
- **The dominance of the generalist cadre;**
- **The integral character of administration in a federal state;**
- **Symmetrical structures of government in the centre and the states;**
- **The centrality of district administration.**

There are many constitutional authorities relevant to the public service such as the C&AG, the UPSC and the state public service commissions, the Finance Commission, the Inter State Council, the Commission for Scheduled Castes and Tribes and administrative tribunals. Some of these, like the C&AG, oversee both levels of government. The Planning Commission is established neither by the Constitution nor by statute, but has functioned as an important agency for formulating and overseeing the process of planned development since 1950 and for recommending the disbursement of Central Plan assistance to states based on objective criteria.

In 2002 there were 50 ministries and over 80 departments, including the President's Secretariat, Cabinet Secretariat and the Prime Minister's office. A number of ministries are divided into two or more departments, each under the charge of a permanent career secretary. The number of ministries and departments and their designation has changed over the years with successive governments and the perceived need to redelineate functions and portfolios. Each ministry or department has a secretariat which assists the government in the tasks of policy formulation, preparation of programmes to translate the policies into action and in ensuring effective execution of policies and programmes, and also assists the Minister to discharge his or her accountability to Parliament. The execution of policies and implementation is entrusted to attached or subordinate offices, autonomous agencies and public sector enterprises subject to review by the Ministry. However, in the case of departmental enterprises like Railways and Posts, the Board is both a secretariat agency and an operating agency linked to a field organisation.

The Permanent Secretary of a department or ministry is usually from the career civil service, mostly under the central staffing scheme, but technical departments are usually headed by civil servants from the technical services or sometimes inducted for fixed terms from the scientific or academic sector. The Secretary is assisted by a hierarchy of officers ranging from the additional and joint secretary to the Director, Deputy Secretary and Under Secretary at supervisory levels. They are in turn supported by a hierarchy of secretariat functionaries ranging from the section officer to assistants, although the scientific departments usually have a non-secretariat structure.

The attached offices may perform different types of activities such as regulatory and investigative functions (Passport Office or Inspector of Factories), development activities (Textile Commissioner), training and education, survey and research, manufacturing and services. The supervisory structure of the attached offices, field offices and heads of departments depends on the nature of the activity, although the offices tend to follow similar secretariat procedures.

Any discussion of public administration in India should extend beyond government departments and field units to consider government-controlled non-departmental units in the central and state administration. These can take the form of autonomous agencies (numbering about 500 in central government), which receive supporting grants or equity capital from the government but appoint their personnel independently. They are usually managed by autonomous boards, although many of them tend to be closely controlled by the ministries. The agencies are engaged in training and research, technological inputs, information technology, industries, commerce, agriculture, arts and culture, and health. The supervising ministries include health and family welfare, women and child welfare, human resources development, culture, science and technology, surface transport, social justice and empowerment, small scale industries, labour, information technology, industry, textiles, commerce, agriculture, urban development and rural development. The agencies are also subject to audit by the C&AG and scrutiny by parliamentary committees. Government recognises the need to improve the oversight of autonomous agencies and increase their accountability.

Besides this arrangement, central and state governments have entrusted on an agency basis to the co-operative sector and user committees specific functions, such as the procurement and marketing of cereals and agricultural commodities, distribution of credit and agricultural inputs to farmers, dairy development, support to handloom weavers and a number of welfare schemes.

The public enterprises form a distinct genre fitting in with the economic ideology of government in the first 40 years of independence. These units, numbering 240 in the year 2000 for central government alone, and many more in the states, undertake a wide variety of manufacturing, service-oriented, developmental, promotional and financing activities, including regional and urban development, industrial estates, house construction and finance. They were initially organised as departmental enterprises like the Railways and Posts, but the structure of most enterprises takes the form of government-owned companies or statutory corporations. These enterprises employ over 2.3 million persons. Central and state governments are engaged in a major programme of reform and privatisation of these enterprises.

Liberalisation of the economy and movements for the protection of consumer interests have led to the growing importance of regulatory authorities in infrastructure and different services, which have been set up under central statute in the field of telecommunications, power, insurance, capital market control and highways. Tribunals have been set up to enable the recovery of loans by banks and financial institutions and for the smooth closure of sick industries. There is a wide spectrum of quasi-judicial tribunals and agencies for adjudication in taxation, excise and customs, labour relations, railways, shipping, transport and drug pricing.

The higher judiciary, in the form of the Supreme Court and state high courts, has played a major role in maintaining constitutional safeguards for the public services, ensuring integrity and promoting meritocracy. It has provided recourse for employees, citizens and business against executive acts of commission and omission. Judicial interpretation has provided a rich case law in civil service matters.

### *Manpower and Services*

In terms of aggregate numbers, India is not particularly overstaffed in comparison with other countries, with total public sector employment at 1.4 per cent of the total population; but this is large as compared with the organised private sector. The public sector in central and state governments, state-owned corporations and local bodies employed 19.1 million persons in 2001, as against 8.6 million in the organised private sector. The problem with the civil service is as much one of affordability as of staff mix, composition, skills, accountability and efficiency.

There were 3.29 million central government employees in March 2002 and they were spread across ministries, departments and their attached offices in Delhi and different parts of the country. This does not include the armed personnel and the members of the judiciary, although they also fall into the broader definition of public servants. The growth rate of staff has come down in aggregate terms, although there has been significant growth in the central police force in recent years.

The public services of central government are broadly classified into the civil services and defence services. The civil services consist of the All India Services and the central civil service. There are three All India Services, which are common to the centre and the states and thus fall under joint control. The central civil services, including the organised services, fall under the control of the central government alone. Except for the central secretariat service, all other supervisory personnel occupy their positions on tenure basis. The Cabinet Secretary is deemed to be the head of the civil service, with the counterpart at state level being the Chief Secretary.

About 86 per cent of the central staff in 2001 was concentrated in the Ministries of Railways (a departmental enterprise), Defence, Posts (a departmental enterprise) and Home Affairs (mainly central police organisations). Artisans and industrial workers constitute one-fifth of the total strength and are covered by laws relating to industrial labour.

Central civil services are governed by the central classification, control and appeal rules, supplemented by the conduct rules, fundamental rules governing pay and allowances, and departmental rules (as in the case of the railways). Regular employees are divided into four groups A to D on the basis of payscales. There is a further grouping into gazetted and non-gazetted categories based on the level of supervisory responsibility and the colonial practice of announcing the appointment and transfer of certain categories of officers in the *Official Gazette*.

The higher civil service in India comprises Group A in policy-making positions and Group B in front-line supervisory and secretariat positions, which are gazetted and form just 7 per cent of the employees. Seventy per cent of the remaining staff work in support positions and front line activities in Group C. Group D consists of artisans and unskilled workers like peons and cleaners with multiple designations in various departments, with an opportunity for vertical movement into Group C positions. Women tend to be under-represented, especially in senior positions. The proportion of staff in Groups C and D range from 99 per cent in railways to 56 per cent in atomic energy. Ironically, this excessive logistical tail often exists alongside significant shortages of staff with skills in information technology, financial management and policy analysis. The members of the central secretariat service occupy the majority of posts in central agencies in Groups B, C and D. The railways have their own secretariat service.

For historical reasons, Indian administration follows the rank-in-person system rather than rank-in-position. Civilian posts are grouped into distinct homogeneous cadres under a common 'service' named on the basis of specific functions attached to the posts in question. A service consists of a group of posts belonging to a distinct functional area and arranged in a hierarchical order representing different grades and rank. A cadre is composed of persons who have been recruited to hold positions requiring similar skills within a service. There are 66 organised services in Groups A and B, of which 21 are non-technical (including revenue, accounts, foreign service and the secretariat), 41 are technical and four belong to central police organisations. Individual ministries, called cadre-controlling authorities, manage one or more services.

Once the person is recruited into a service, he or she moves up the hierarchy of posts in different grades and is liable to be transferred among posts in the service with a similar grade regardless of the nature of their function. The central staffing scheme provides the structure for the induction of members of the AIS and central services in different secretariat posts on the basis of empanelment and selection for higher posts. Once empanelled in positions ranging from the Deputy Secretary to Permanent Secretary, the officer could be assigned to work in any ministry or central organisation with due regard for past experience and current skills for the duration of the officer's tenure.

The growth of central services has been incremental and the numbers keep changing as some of the services are reconstituted. A central civil service is recruited and controlled by the central government while the members of All India Services are recruited by the central government but jointly controlled by the central and state governments. The size of a service varies according to functional requirements. Periodic cadre reviews aim to address stagnation and changes in functions, even as the finance and personnel ministries look more broadly at rightsizing and equity in career opportunities of employees across cadres.

These are the Indian Administrative Service (IAS), Indian Police Service (IPS) and Indian Forest Service (IFOS). They constitute the senior executive services of administration besides such important central services as the foreign service, audit and accounts, central revenues, railways and engineering. There is dual control over the AIS with the concerned central ministries having the final word in disciplinary matters, emoluments and promotion. The members of IAS occupy most of the top management posts in the central and state administrations.

Besides regular pensionable staff, there is a large number of casual and temporary staff in many ministries as well as technical and other staff employed against project funds. Since 1986 there has been a ban on the appointment of work-charged employees and existing employees are being progressively absorbed into vacant pensionable posts. This type of temporary employment should be distinguished from the outsourcing of housekeeping, security and other non-core services in different departments as there workers are employed by contractors.

### *State Services*

There are about 7.5 million employees in state governments. The state civil services are composed of general cadres and a large number of functional services in different sectors. As in central government, the state civil service is categorised into four groups or grades, out of which the top two classes form the numerically smaller group but comprise the executive and supervisory levels. There are excessive numbers of employees in clerical positions in Group C at the same time as a serious shortage of persons in critical front line positions such as police, teachers and health staff. Yet, varying cadre rules and the tradition of 'a job for life' often make it difficult to terminate the employment of redundant staff or to transfer surplus staff to areas where there is a higher demand.

There are many technical and non-technical services in the states, as in central government, and the number has grown by growth of services and cadres over the years. The pattern of secretariat administration in states is largely similar to that in central government. The departments are supported by heads of departments and directors of field establishments. The district administration is responsible for many basic functions, including land administration, law and order and basic services. Any discussion of state administration should note the differences between the AIS and state cadres in respect of independence and liability to political interference and disciplinary action.

There are about 2.3 million employees in local government in rural and urban areas, but the pattern and terms of employment and the nature of cadres vary between states. Municipal corporations have been set up for larger cities. Some states have constituted local cadres of development staff under the control of elected local bodies. The advent of democratic decentralisation has also witnessed the practice of teachers and health staff being under the oversight of local citizen committees and panchayats.

### *Personnel Management and Establishment Control*

The responsibility for establishment control is divided among the Department of Expenditure in the Ministry of Finance and the Ministry of Personnel, Pensions and Public Grievances (PPPG), especially the Department of Personnel and Training (DOPT). Both departments jointly decide issues relating to pay and allowances and terminal benefits, matters arising out of the recommendations of pay commissions, control over staff size and the redeployment of surplus staff. In practice, control over central government staff is fragmented among ministries, with just four Ministries, namely Railways, Defence, Home and Posts (and Telecommunications till its corporatisation) being responsible for about 86 per cent of staff and dealing with operational matters.

The Ministry of PPGP is the co-ordinating agency in the central government for personnel matters, especially recruitment, training, career development, staff welfare, terminal benefits, public grievances and administrative reforms. It administers a number of statutory organisations and other agencies including the UPSC, training institutes and the Central Vigilance Commissioner. The Ministry is under a single permanent secretary but consists of the SIS Department of Personnel and Training, Department of Administrative Reforms and Public Grievances (ARPG) and the Department of Pensions and Pensioner Welfare (DPPW). The DPPW is the nodal department for all matters relating to central government pensions and the welfare of a vast group of civilian pensioners, and the department also handles matters relating to central secretariat service and surplus staff.

The Department of Administrative Reforms and Public Grievances aims to facilitate the pursuit of excellence in governance through promotion of improvements in government structures and processes, citizen-friendly initiatives including redress of public grievances, documentation, incubation and dissemination of best practices, codification and simplification of procedures and networking with various agencies. It also supports the efforts of the Cabinet Secretariat and Prime Minister's office to guide reforms in administration.

At a more immediate level, DOPT has the direct responsibility of being the cadre controlling authority for the IAS and the Central Secretariat Service (CSS). The Department also operates the Central Staffing Scheme under which suitable officers from the AIS and the Group A Central Services are selected and then placed in post at the level of deputy secretary/director and joint secretary on the basis of tenure deputation. The department also deals with cases of appointments to posts of chairman, managing director, full-time functional director/member of the boards of management of various public sector undertakings and enterprises, corporations, banks and financial institutions.

### *Recruitment*

The Indian Constitution envisages that the central parliament or the appropriate state legislature may regulate the recruitment and conditions of service of persons appointed to public services and posts in connection with the affairs of the Union or of any state. However, the central and state governments have not enacted a comprehensive law for the civil service and have been content to regulate service matters by rules.

The Constitution envisages reservation of government posts for socially disadvantaged groups, namely scheduled castes, scheduled tribes and other backward classes, as a part of a package of affirmative action for these groups to improve their social status and economic well-being. The Commission for Scheduled Castes and Tribes supervises measures for their welfare and legal steps to prevent discrimination against members of these groups.

Apart from the scheme of reservation for socially disadvantaged groups, central and state governments have been following a policy of reserving up to 5 per cent of the posts, especially in Groups C and D, for compassionate appointment of the spouse and dependent heirs of deceased government servants. The appointees may not fulfil all the qualifications for the post, but in order to qualify must face penurious conditions.

Article 309 of the Constitution requires that every post should have recruitment rules, which specify the name of the post, payscale, mode of recruitment and the recruiting authority, whether it is through UPSC or any other source. The same procedure is applicable to state governments which have their own State Public Service Commission for recruitment and promotion to state level posts. The public sector units and autonomous agencies have their own recruitment rules and machinery although the nationalised banks have operated a centralised recruiting system for many years. While the local bodies under state governments are usually allowed to recruit Group C and D personnel, the higher cadres tend to be centralised and controlled by state governments except in few states.

For the three All India Services and the organised services in Groups A and B, entry is by direct recruitment and entry into all higher levels is by promotion and selection. Lower and upper age limits have been prescribed for appointment to organised services and individual posts, with relaxation for scheduled castes and tribes. The recruitment rules for organised services lay down *inter alia* the grades of the service, authorised strength, initial constitution of the service and its future maintenance, appointment to the service, probation, seniority, disqualification, etc. In respect of posts not covered by any organised service, the recruitment rules are notified in a Schedule with 14 columns according to guidelines issued by the Ministry of Personnel. DOPT advises the departments to update the rules or frame new rules for isolated posts following revision of pay scales and service conditions or in the light of technological change or work norms or functional reorganisation. The departments have been advised to simplify the rules and retain only core requirements since prolix rules become the subject of litigation. It is proposed to phase out the lowest clerical levels and commence recruitment from computer-literate assistants.

All proposals for senior appointments under the Government of India, which require the approval of the Appointments Committee of the Cabinet (ACC) are processed through the Establishment Officer in the Ministry of Personnel as Secretary of the ACC. These include board level appointments to central public sector undertakings and appointments of joint secretaries, directors and deputy secretaries in the ministries and departments. The Cabinet Secretariat prepares the panels for appointment as secretaries and additional secretaries with the approval of the ACC.

### *Recruiting Agencies*

In the constitutional scheme, public service commissions are primarily recruiting authorities and have an advisory role in rules and disciplinary matters. They have no active part in personnel management, unlike some other Commonwealth countries. Appointments are made by various departments according to rules of delegation.

Recruitment at Grade B and Grade A levels, whether through direct recruitment or promotion, generally takes place at UPSC level through 12 examinations covering civilian and armed forces posts, together with technical jobs like doctors, telecom engineers, geologists, etc. Grade C non-technical posts are filled through the Staff Selection Commission (SSC) which has various branches. Recruitment to railway posts at Grade C and D levels takes place through Railway Recruitment Boards which have 19 branches all over the country. In addition, agricultural scientists and defence scientists in atomic energy have their own arrangement for recruitment and promotion. The Postal Department and the Telecom Department fill Group D posts through recruitment at their own level, but the bulk of recruitment in central government at the lowest level, Group D, takes place through employment exchanges. In these cases the employment exchange sponsors candidates to fill vacancies but posts can also be filled through publication in *Employment News*.

The two organisations through which the government ensures merit-based recruitment of personnel for the government are the Union Public Service Commission and the Staff Selection Commission. The UPSC is constituted under provisions of the Constitution with considerable independence and informs the legislature annually about its activities and areas of disagreement with government. It consists of a chairperson and ten members, who are assisted by a large secretariat. It is responsible for conducting examinations and interviews for appointment to the higher civil services and civil posts under the Union Government, including recruitment to the All India Services and organised Group A services. In effect, the number of posts in respect of whom recruitment rules are to be framed in consultation with the UPSC is less than 5 per cent of all government posts, but these posts constitute the decision-making levels.

Unlike the UPSC the SSC is constituted by executive order, but it has considerable autonomy. It is responsible for recruiting subordinate staff in all organisations, except railways and the C&AG, including assistants, stenographers and many Group B (with pay less than Rs. 10,500) and Group C posts through competitive examination and interviews.

Individual ministries have set up recruitment boards for non-gazetted posts such as the 19 railways regional recruitment boards and the committees under the Home Ministry for recruiting paramilitary personnel. Group D employees are usually recruited at departmental level through applications from persons registered with the employment exchange.

The public sector undertakings are categorised under four schedules. The Public Enterprises Selection Board (PESB) is an executive agency entrusted with responsibility for inviting applications and making recommendations for appointment to full-time board level posts for the posts of Chief Executive, functional directors and part-time chairperson in public sector undertakings. The PESB also advises government on senior management personnel, their performance appraisal and training in these enterprises.

### *Pay and Benefits Policy*

The pay, allowances and various benefits of employees are periodically determined by the government on the basis of the recommendations of pay commissions (usually appointed every ten years), followed by negotiation with recognised employee unions. The principles which determine the rate of pay are inclusiveness, comprehensiveness, model employer, pay in private sector and adequacy. The compression ratio between the top and bottom posts has been falling since the 1980s. The Fifth Central Pay Commission (FCPC) provided for 100 per cent neutralisation of inflation for all personnel through dearness allowance. The report of the Fifth Central Pay Commission (1996) led to generous formulae for pay determination, and terminal benefits and allowances, and for a substantial increase in expenditure on salaries and pensions.

Apart from basic pay, major allowances and benefits include dearness allowance, house rent and city compensatory allowance and a host of other allowances. Terminal benefits include pension, gratuity, encashment of accumulated leave, balance in contributory provident fund and group insurance. Family pension up to a maximum of 30 per cent of basic pay is paid to the spouse of deceased employees. There are at present an average of seven pensioners for each serving employee. Alarmed by the growing burden of pensions, the central government has introduced a contributory pension scheme for all future employees.

### *Promotion*

Different criteria are adopted for the promotion of employees to higher posts depending on the group. Government seeks to ensure the merit principle through the preparation of panels by departmental promotion committees (DPCs) after assessing the confidential rolls and reports of integrity and disciplinary proceedings. The seniority principle is generally respected. The procedure is subject to reservation for posts up to Group A for persons belonging to scheduled castes and tribes.

The assured career progression (ACP) scheme is intended to deal with the problem of stagnation and provides automatic movement to the higher scale for employees other than those in group A after the stages of 12 and 24 years; this is not construed as regular promotion. The scientific ministries are allowed to operate a scheme of flexible complementing to enable a scientist to move to higher grade on the basis of merit.

### *Performance Assessment*

Although supervisors have an opportunity for continuous feedback from employees and for guidance, the chief instrument for formal appraisal is the Annual Confidential Report (ACR). The ACR is designed to improve the performance of the official and enhance his or her capacity to contribute to organisational goals, while assessing their potential and preparing them through feedback, guidance and training for further advancement. The ACR is used at various times to screen the performance of the employee for the purpose of promotion, ACP or placement and for reviewing the need for continuation in service.

There are different formats for AIS, gazetted officers and non-gazetted staff with variations introduced by technical departments. The grade assigned by the reporting officer, ranging from poor to outstanding, is subject to review at one or two levels. Some scientific ministries and army grade officers are on a ten-point scale.

### *Disciplinary Proceedings*

Besides liability for prosecution under the Prevention of Corruption Act for corrupt behaviour, departmental enquiries can be initiated by individual departments or the DOPT against regular employees for misconduct and lack of probity. The rules of enquiry and for punishment are subject to constitutional protection against arbitrary dismissal or punishment. Major punishments include dismissal, demotion and removal, while minor disciplinary measures include stoppage of increment and censure. The disciplinary authority is required to consult the UPSC and Central Vigilance Commissioner (CVC) in cases involving Group A employees and other designated officers before a final decision is made on punishment. The employee has the right of appeal to government or to take their case to the Central Administrative Tribunal (CAT) or the High Court.

## 2.3 Efforts at Administrative Reform

It was realised during the early years after independence that the colonial system of administration was not suited for the enormous challenges of democratic development and federalism. A milestone in the history of administrative reform in India was the establishment of the Administrative Reforms Commission (ARC) in 1966 and its reports on various aspects of central, state and local administration. The most important reports were on the machinery of government, planning machinery, state and district administration, economic and financial administration, personnel administration and redress of public grievances. Its recommendations led to the establishment of the Department of Personnel, the strengthening of the Department for Administrative Reforms, and the constitution of cells for organisation and management (O&M) in different departments.

Various expert committees, including central pay commissions have provided advice over the years on the machinery of government and civil service. The National Police Commission enquired into all aspects of police administration in 1977. It was the first commission to deal with the vexed issue of political interference in the placement and promotion of police officers and recommended an institutionalised solution. The state governments also set up commissions to consider administrative reforms and expert committees to suggest improvements in all or specific aspects of administration. The institutional structure for tackling corruption has evolved in parallel, signified by the statute setting up the office Central Vigilance Commissioner and establishing Vigilance Commissions, ombudsmen and anti-corruption bureaux in the states.

# 3 Human Resource Management

## 3.1 Ensuring Merit and Non-discrimination in Human Resource Management

Building a motivated and capable civil service requires merit-based and non-discriminatory recruitment, which rests on the absence of political patronage, transparent rules and procedures, open competition and selection by an independent agency. Subsequent to recruitment, important elements in meritocracy and the motivation of employees are emoluments, opportunities for promotion, recognition and reward for performance, inter-sector mobility, placement in the right jobs, and scope for skill upgrading and self-improvement. Government considers it equally important to address demotivating factors like frequent and arbitrary transfers, a poor work environment, decrepit housing and health facilities, as well as special factors affecting women in office and field jobs.

There are constitutional provisions for establishing central and state public service commissions, the All India Services and administrative tribunals. The chairperson and members of the public service commissions enjoy security of tenure and government respects the autonomy and advice of the Commission. The members cannot be removed except in accordance with the procedure prescribed in the Constitution. Other recruiting agencies, such as the Service Selection Commission, do not enjoy constitutional protection but operate with considerable independence in practice. The candidates for different posts up to Group C are selected on the basis of competitive examinations followed in most cases by interview. The Supreme Court has consistently upheld the merit principle and has observed that compassionate appointment is an exception to this general rule.

The UPSC has been successful in maintaining the merit principle in direct recruitment and selection for senior posts, except for its adherence to the rules for reservation. It has a limited role in personnel management and diverse policies for recruitment and placement except to the extent specified in rules. Thus, the initiative for enforcing the merit principle comes primarily from the central and state governments. The departments in charge of personnel and individual services are responsible for the enforcement of merit-based procedures and practices at all stages of career progression after entry into the service.

Members of public services have always been concerned about the differential in salaries and perquisites in comparison with the private sector. This concern has been reflected in the reports of successive pay commissions. Government has endeavoured to reduce the differential, but the reduction of tensions over inter-service career prospects has proved difficult in practice.

The Constitution assures security of tenure to government servants and provides them with protection from arbitrary punishment, dismissal and removal from service or reduction in rank except after reasonable opportunity and due process. The government is required to consult the Public Service Commission before imposing punishment on officers belonging to Group A. This constitutional right is elaborated in service rules. The right to due process under law and the rules is enforceable through administrative tribunals, High Courts and the Supreme Court, as thousands of cases in the last 40 years demonstrate.

In the final assessment, promotion – with its higher emoluments and enhanced status – remains a key element of motivation. The preparation of panels by constituted committees for promotion to various posts is based on transparent rules, performance assessment reports, integrity of the employee and adherence to published seniority lists. Rules for promotion tend to assign greater weight to seniority for Groups C and D and to seniority cum merit for gazetted positions, with the empanelment process guiding the selection of officers as deputy secretaries and above. Unlike merit assessed on the basis of performance, the number of years of service is the only criterion, which is less subject to manipulation by vested interests. It seems important, on balance, to give a progressively important role to merit considerations in promotion, especially for higher posts, but to do this with reference to improvements in performance appraisal and employees' perceptions of the fairness and consistency of the process.

More critical in terms of effect on employee morale are the instances of arbitrary and frequent transfer of employees in state governments and their effect on work ethic and morale. Recent reforms in transfer policy in central and state government deal with the problems facing central and state services by laying down minimum tenures for posts and by institutionalising the process through mechanisms like the Civil Services Board to uphold the merit principle. Another reform at the centre attempts to avoid the scope for collusive behaviour to obtain extension in service or re-employment and to ban the provision of extension in service for all civil servants except for the grant of fixed tenure to the Cabinet Secretary.

**_Box 3.1_ Meritocracy in States**

**The policy statements on civil service reform in states like Uttar Pradesh, Andhra Pradesh, Karnataka and Orissa reflect the proposed steps to improve meritocracy through reforms in the recruitment process and in performance evaluation, publicising and rewarding good performance, and implementing a comprehensive training plan to upgrade skills and quality. Besides periodic increases in pay and allowances, the state governments are experimenting with a variety of incentives to promote greater motivation and to reward good performance at middle and senior levels. The incentives for senior officers include selection for posts in international, public and voluntary organisations with higher allowances and preferred job content, opportunity for advanced studies and training in India and abroad. The incentives, which are common to all employees, include cash awards, advance increments, department-wide awards for best performance, and public recognition and out-of-turn promotion for Groups C and D in some cases.**

### *Non-Discrimination and Reservation in Posts*

The Indian Constitution prohibits discrimination against any citizen based on religion, race, caste, region, language and gender. The legal provisions for recruitment and promotion are designed to ensure selection of candidates without any discrimination on the basis of any extraneous criteria and the use of the merit principle for the selection of candidates. At the same time, as in some Commonwealth countries, efforts have been made to correct the effects of past discrimination through constitutional provisions for affirmative action and quotas in favour of socially disadvantaged groups in recruitment and promotion.

The main objective of providing reservations for scheduled castes and scheduled tribes in civil posts and government services is to increase their representation in the services and facilitate their social and economic advancement. Reservation is supported on the ground of making the public service truly representative of the socio-economic composition of the population, consistent with the maintenance of efficiency of administration in the making of appointments to posts and services. Government is not required to consult the UPSC/state Public Service Commission (PSC) in making reservations. A recent amendment to the Constitution empowers government to make reservation in matters of promotion in any class of service or posts.

Various instructions have been issued by government on the basis of these constitutional provisions to provide for reservation in services for members of the Scheduled Castes (SC), Scheduled Tribes (ST) and Other Backward Classes (OBC) by following a roster system. Reservation for these groups is available in all posts including the All India Services in case of direct recruitment subject to the limit of 50 per cent of the posts and a limit of 27 per cent for OBC. While in the case of direct recruitment on an all India basis by open competition, the reservation for SC, ST and OBC is respectively 15 per cent, 7.5 per cent and 27 per cent, the percentages are 16.66 per cent, 7.5 per cent and 25.84 per cent respectively in case of direct recruitment otherwise than by open competition. Reservation in promotion by non-selection is available to members of SC and ST in all the groups of services at the rate of 15 per cent and 7.5 per cent respectively. In case of promotion by the selection method, reservation for SC and ST is available up to the lowest rung of Group A at the same percentages. There is no reservation for OBC in promotion.

Various concessions are available to improve the chances of representation of SC and ST in services. These include relaxation in the upper age limit, unlimited chances within the modified age limit for appearing in competitive examinations, exemption from payment of examination fees, relaxation of standards of suitability, non-adjustment of persons selected on their own merit against reserved vacancies, provision of carry-forward of vacancies, exchange of vacancies between SC and ST, etc. OBC candidates enjoy concessions in relation to the modification of the upper age limit and concessions in relation to the number of times they can take examinations. Consequential seniority is available to SC and ST employees who are promoted by virtue of rule of reservation. The selection committees contain representatives from women and the reserved groups. Liaison officers have been appointed in each ministry to ensure compliance with the rules and instructions relating to reservation for SC, ST and OBC.

The state governments have issued rules to reserve posts for the scheduled castes and tribes in proportion to their presence in the total population of the state and for reservation of posts for OBC within the total permissible percentage of 50 per cent of posts. The percentage of reservation varies among states. Rules also provide for various safeguards and rosters similar to those in central government.

Some state governments practice a policy of reservation of posts at the lower level for candidates belonging to the state to encourage local employment. One southern state has declared posts in Groups C and D as falling in district and regional cadres, and these posts are reserved for persons coming from the district and region. This measure is a politically acceptable concession to regional aspirations in the context of varying levels of development within large states in a historical context, and is not seen as undermining the merit principle.

### *Compassionate Appointment and Special Categories*

There is a provision for compassionate employment with a reservation in direct recruitment up to 5 per cent for legal heirs of deceased employees and reservation of 10 per cent in certain Group C and D vacancies for ex-servicemen, but within the overall limit of 50 per cent. Under separate legislation for persons with disabilities, every appropriate government is required to appoint to not less than 3 per cent of posts in each establishment persons with disabilities such as blindness, hearing impairment and other specified disabilities. Reservation for groups such as ex-servicemen, the physically handicapped, project-displaced families and legal heirs of deceased employees is available in central and state governments; this is termed horizontal reservation. By contrast, the reservation for socially disadvantaged groups is termed vertical reservation.

Many see the provision for compassionate appointment of dependents of deceased employees in Groups C and D as undermining the principle of merit-based appointment, as eligibility requirements are often relaxed for these candidates. This is particularly so because generous pensions are available for the spouse and dependent members of deceased employees. Some states are making a move towards phasing out this form of appointment.

### *Gender Issues*

The principle of gender equality is enshrined in the Constitution and civil service rules. Central government conducted a detailed survey in 1997 to assess perceptions of departmental heads and employees from both genders. It was found that there is a consistent under-representation of women in different levels of the civil service, especially Groups A and B, despite equal opportunity for entry into the public service. The glass ceiling appears to operate for the appointment of women in important ministries.

The Central Ministry of PPGP has undertaken an initiative to sensitise various cadre-controlling authorities to the need to open up recruitment opportunities for women and address their problems of career development and placement in the higher civil services. Greater publicity is car given to encourage women to apply for various positions. Women are generally posted in the her same place as their spouses as far as possible. Women are given equality of treatment in accommodation and house building loans. Day care centres for children and women's rest rooms are available in secretariat offices. An institutional mechanism in the form of networked nodal officers in different ministries, anchored by the DOPT, is being devised to examine women's issues in the civil services and to expedite action on complaints received from women employees. Following directions of the Supreme Court, the civil service rules have been amended to deal with and punish incidents of harassment of women employees in the workplace. The progress of various measures is periodically reviewed by a Steering Committee under the chairmanship of the Secretary, Ministry of PPGP.

A number of state governments have been as progressive as the central government. The problems of women employees working in districts and blocks with fewer facilities for health, education and housing have engaged the attention of governments. Women officers have occupied the position of chief secretaries and secretaries of important departments like finance. While there is no quota for women candidates in the central government, states like Karnataka and Andhra Pradesh have reserved one-third of posts for women within the overall scheme of reservation.

## 3.2 Recruitment Policy and Practices

The legal structure of the public service provides for lifetime employment for most regular employees up to the age of superannuation, which is 60 in central government and 58 or 60 in the states. The Indian Constitution envisages that the central parliament or the appropriate state legislature should regulate by law the recruitment and conditions of service of persons appointed to public services and posts in connection with the affairs of the Union or of any state. However, barring laws in limited areas of central and state administration, the central and state governments have not enacted a comprehensive law for the civil service. The recruitment and service conditions of the public service are mainly regulated by rules notified by central and state governments in respect of employees working under them. The recruitment rules/service rules notified by the President under a proviso to Article 309 of the Constitution are legally enforceable.

There are at present 66 organised services besides the AIS. There are many unorganised services with clusters of posts for which special rules are framed. All of them, except some of the scientific ministries, are organised into four groups A to D according to pay scales and levels of responsibility in the classification laid down by the DOPT and Ministry of Finance. The members of the central secretariat service occupy the majority of posts in the central agencies, especially Groups B, C and D. The Ministry of Railways has its own secretariat service.

The departments make appointment according to rules of delegation, once the list of candidates is received from the Public Service Commission or other recruitment agencies. The appointment of candidates to the Indian Administrative Service, the premier generalist service, is made by the DOPT to different state cadres. The appointment of a government servant to a permanent post may be substantive or on probation or on an officiating basis. A substantive appointment to a permanent post normally confers a substantive right to the post called a 'lien'.

### *Recruitment Practice*

Recruitment is a comprehensive term and includes any method provided for inducting a person into the public service. The diverse modes of recruitment and appointment in the civil service include direct recruitment, promotion, transfer, deputation and contract appointment. Since 100 per cent promotion is the primary method of recruitment following initial entry in respect of posts included in a service, other methods such as lateral entry and contract appointment are resorted to only in specified circumstances for which explicit provisions are to be made in the rules. The induction of persons from the private sector into government is considered selectively in technical organisations.

The qualification for direct and the other various methods of recruitment is decided by the cadre controlling authority in consultation with DOPT and the UPSC (where specified), based on the duties and responsibilities of the post and the entire cadre structure. Recruitment for most posts involves competitive examinations and interviews, although the railways and several states have abolished interview for lower posts to reduce the subjective element. In respect of posts not covered by any organised service, the recruitment rules are notified in a Schedule with 14 columns according to guidelines issued by the Ministry of Personnel.

The lower age limit for recruitment to the AIS and central services is 21 to 28 years, but the upper age limit can be relaxed by up to five years for candidates belonging to the reserved groups. While general candidates have four chances to appear for the examination, there are no limits for candidates from SC and ST who fall within the age limit. Candidates with a general or professional degree from any of the recognised universities or technical institutions can apply for these examinations.

### *Problems in Recruitment*

The Fifth Central Pay Commission (FCPC) and other expert committees have commented on the delay and deficiencies of the present process of recruitment and selection, though UPSC has a distinguished record of prompt declaration of results. Remedial steps by the SSC have reduced delays in recruitment and the Commission has also increased the period of validity of the panel.

The present recruitment process, especially in the states, suffers from outdated rules, delay in the initiation of action by the departments, difficulties faced by recruiting agencies and delays in completion of medical examinations and verification of character. All these problems lead to delays in securing competent candidates in time to fill critical vacancies and force departments to make ad hoc arrangements to perform the work. Often, posts cannot be filled in the states for want of recruitment rules or litigation. The process is also beset by litigation in respect of examinations, reservation issues and interpretation of the rules.

### *Lateral Entry and Mobility*

The service rules, as well as the recruitment rules for isolated posts, provide, among other methods of recruitment, for lateral entry into the service. In the recruitment rules for the general central service, absorption, transfer on deputation, short-term contracts, etc. are prescribed as methods of recruitment depending on the cadre structure, the qualification and functional requirements of the post and availability of suitable officers in the feeder grades. Re-employment of retired persons is increasingly being discouraged by central government and some states. The UPSC is consulted in respect of recruitment by selection or lateral entry for Group A services.

The rules for AIS, and many central services do not envisage lateral recruitment at levels higher than the entry post or one level above. Even in the CSS and Railways, entry by selection into junior management posts is limited to internal candidates. In most states, recruitment for secretariat positions is possible only at the lowest level and not at higher levels such as section officers and under-secretary.

As they are less hierarchically organised, the scientific ministries have resorted to lateral entry more liberally. The central government, and to a lesser extent the states, have followed the practice of appointing reputed academics and experts in a particular field as members of planning commissions or as secretaries of technical ministries. The recruitment rules in central government permit lateral recruitment to technical positions of advisers at the grade of directors to additional secretaries in the Planning Commission and ministries such as the Ministries of Railways, Telecommunications, Industry and Petroleum. However, such recruitment accounts for a small proportion of total strength. The bureaucracy does not see this mode of entry as a structural change in the hierarchy of functional and generalist services.

There are differing opinions on the extent to which the administration benefits from the entry of outsiders, based on the performance of outside entrants in short- or long-term assignments. The really competent outsiders have been deterred by the exclusion of lateral entrants from the policy-making process and the lesser attraction of public service with its below-market pay and constraining work environment. The ARC cautioned government in 1967 about the need to ensure that the skills which the lateral entrants were expected to bring in were not already available within the civil service. It is necessary to avoid the risk that the selection process becomes arbitrary and demoralises serving personnel to an extent that far outweighs the likely benefits from lateral entry.

As regards mobility of the services, there is provision in the organised Group A services for entry of officers serving in other departments through the methods of deputation or absorption. The members of IAS can freely move within any of the cadre posts and can be posted to public sector undertakings on deputation. Once selected for the post of deputy secretary and above, the members of organised services and AIS can be appointed to any post under the central staffing scheme during their central tenure.

Mobility can extend outside government service as well. The governments of Kerala and West Bengal have enabling rules for permitting government servants to take leave, continuously or in broken periods, for up to 15 years to take up alternative employment in India or abroad. The Maharashtra government has introduced a scheme of extraordinary leave up to five years for government employees (other than teachers, doctors, nurses and police). During this leave period, employees are allowed to take up employment outside government provided they have had no official dealings with the new employer in the last five years. This period is treated as duty for all purposes, including seniority and retirement benefits. The cadre strength of the employee concerned is reduced and the resultant vacancy is not be filled during the leave period.

### *Contract Appointments*

Generally, recruitment to posts which are likely to continue beyond one year, are made on a regular basis and the UPSC has to be consulted for filling such positions on ad hoc basis. Appointments on contract are generally not resorted to except in a few jobs requiring specialisation or for temporary projects. A contract appointment is one where an employee signs a legal contract to perform assigned tasks for a specified period on agreed terms and conditions. The employee is not entitled to the constitutional protection available for regular employees except when his/her services are prematurely terminated without due process. A form of appointment for temporary work that is widely prevalent is the engagement of consultants (drawn from retired officials and experts) to handle specialised (and not regular) jobs for a period not exceeding one year.

However, a number of central ministries, state governments and training institutions are exploring alternatives to lifetime employment, such as contract employment for specialised jobs, so as to maintain flexibility in the staffing pattern. Such recruitment is often exempted from the purview of the PSC. The Committee on Recruitment Rules recommended that in order to attract the best talent within and outside the country for scientific and other specialised posts, provision for contract appointment might be made in addition to the present method of direct recruitment or deputation At the same time, a number of state governments and central ministries are apprehensive about the possible abuse of the system of contract appointment for political and bureaucratic patronage, and about the risk of regularisation of such appointees.

### *Central Recruiting Agencies – the UPSC and SSC*

The two organisations through which the government ensures recruitment of personnel for the Government are the Union Public Service Commission and the Staff Selection Commission. The former is a constitutional authority while the latter is set up by an executive order.

In the constitutional scheme, public service commissions are primarily modelled on the practice of insulating the process of recruitment to the public service from political patronage and favouritism. A wider mandate for the PSCs was not intended in the Constitution nor is it envisaged in the set of reforms which are now before the government. The Commissions have a primarily advisory role in the framing of recruitment rules, selection of persons at post-entry level and disciplinary matters. They have no active part in personnel management, unlike in some other Commonwealth countries. In addition to posts in Groups C and D, state governments often exclude posts in gazetted services and technical cadres such as health and engineering from the purview of PSCs under the plea of delays and excessive workload of the Commission.

The UPSC is constituted under provisions of the Constitution with considerable independence and submits an annual report to Parliament about its activities and areas of disagreement with government. The Commission consists of a chairperson and ten members, who are assisted by a professional secretariat. The members are chosen carefully from a pool of reputable persons from the fields of academic science, the civil service, army and civil society with due regard for the representation of women. In order to reinforce their impartiality, members are debarred from future employment in central or state government after a fixed tenure of six years or the age of 67 years, whichever is earlier. The Commission is assisted by a professional staff headed by a secretary and is provided with adequate funds for its activities.

There is a mandatory provision for consulting the Commission on all matters relating to methods of recruitment for Group A and B services, principles to be followed in making promotions and transfers from one service to another and on all disciplinary matters affecting persons in the central and state administrations, on claims for the award of pensions and on costs incurred in defending legal proceedings in respect of actions performed in the course of duty. Members of the UPSC preside over the committees for promotion to the AIS from state services, and over the committees for promotion for each service from Group B to Group A and from one grade to another in Group A. The advice of the UPSC is generally considered mandatory and government is very careful about recording disagreement with the Commission.

In terms of a proviso to clause (3) of Article 320 of the Constitution, the President has made regulations called the Union Public Service Commission (Exemption from Consultation) Regulations, 1958. The UPSC is not required to be consulted on matters relating to methods of recruitment and principles to be followed in making appointments to Groups C and D services and posts or to certain scientific organisations. The UPSC is also not consulted on the empanelment for senior positions in the AIS, Group A central services and armed forces. Due to these regulations, only around 5 per cent of government posts under fall within the purview of the Commission. The exempted posts include posts which fall under the Department of Atomic Energy, Department of Space, DRDO, other scientific organisations such as the Department of Science and Technology and the Department of Biotechnology, posts under the intelligence agencies and posts attached to constitutional authorities. The UPSC has been jealous about further encroachments on its authority and has been advocating the need for consultation on recruitment practices at least for all gazetted services.

The SSC is constituted by executive order but is granted considerable autonomy. It is responsible for recruiting subordinate staff such as assistants, stenographers and many posts in Group B (with pay less than Rs. 10,500) and Group C through competitive examinations and interviews. Group D employees are usually recruited at departmental level through interviews of candidates sent by the government-controlled employment exchange with reservation of up to 5 per cent of vacancies for the dependents of deceased employees.

As a principle of merit-based recruitment since colonial times, the selection of eligible candidates for posts up to Group C is through competitive examination at the All India level for central services, whether by the UPSC or SSC or the recruitment boards of individual ministries. A wide variety of eligibility requirements, experience and professional qualifications are prescribed, depending on the nature of the post and the service. For examinations leading to appointment to gazetted central civil services, a graduate degree is mandatory. This is followed by interview of candidates, who are short-listed on the basis of marks in the examination. There is a provision for region-wide applications and selection in respect of CSS and regional cadres.

While the number of posts for direct recruitment by the UPSC and SSC has declined in recent years due to economy measures, there has been a huge increase in the number of applicants (about 2.5 million for the SSC). The SSC has outsourced many of its activities in order to ensure the prompt declaration of results. The UPSC has computerised the screening and processing of examination and recruitment applications to reduce the processing time and to minimise errors. It has used innovative methods and competent evaluators for the evaluation of objective and descriptive papers, which are produced in 19 languages.

Government, employees and the public respect the integrity and independence of the UPSC in ensuring merit-based recruitment and promotion and in providing a measure of protection against arbitrary decisions in disciplinary matters. Expert committees have deliberated on the UPSC system of selection of candidates for senior executive services and an expert committee under Professor Alagh has reported recently on further improvements. This report is under consideration.

### *Box 3.2* The UPSC and Examinations

**Recruitment for the senior executive service and Groups A and B levels, defence personnel, and technical jobs such doctors, telecom engineers and geologists, whether through direct recruitment or selection, generally takes place at UPSC level through examinations covering civilian and defence personnel, followed by interview. The Commission conducts over 12 examinations each year in 42 centres. A common application form with a single sheet has been devised for all the examinations to make the form susceptible to quick computerised scanning. A common All India examination is conducted for the AIS and central services in two stages, first a qualifying preliminary examination and then a main examination in eight chosen subjects for the short-listed candidates. There is a separate examination for the IFOS. The candidates are allowed to write the main examination in any one of the 19 major languages. The qualifying candidates are then called for interview in selected centres. Outside experts are associated with the interview. The final grading includes marks obtained in the examination and interview, and the candidates are ranked for allocation to the IAS, IPS and general services according to their preference, with due regard to the reservation quota and criteria.**

### *Other Agencies*

Individual central ministries have set up recruitment boards for posts in Groups C and D such as the 19 railway regional recruitment boards and the committees for recruiting paramilitary personnel under the Home Ministry. In addition, ministries have their own arrangements of independent boards or committees for recruitment and promotion of agricultural scientists, defence scientists and technical personnel in the Departments of Atomic Energy and Space outside the UPSC. The PESB is an executive agency entrusted with responsibility for inviting applications and making recommendations for appointment to full-time board level posts for the posts of chief executive and functional directors and part-time chairpersons in public sector undertakings. The public sector units have their own recruitment arrangements though the rules are usually vetted by the controlling departments.

In the case of Group D employees (both skilled and unskilled), the Postal Department and the Telecom Department fill posts through recruitment at their level, but the bulk of recruitment to central government takes place through employment exchanges. In such cases the employment exchange sponsors candidates for filling the vacancies, but posts can also be filled through publication in *Employment News* which is published in Hindi, English and Urdu. Generally, six weeks notice is given before the vacancies are filled.

### State Governments

The state governments adopt similar procedures for state or district level services, depending on the nature of the department or the function. As in the case of railways, states such as Karnataka have abolished the interview of candidates for Group C posts in order to eliminate the scope for bias. The state PSCs perform tasks similar to those of the UPSC and enjoy constitutional authority. However, their independence and credibility are less assured in some states and many posts are withdrawn from their purview under the plea of delays in recruitment. The state PSCs also suffer from inadequate support in the form of staff and resources and this often leads to delays in the declaration of results. The exclusion of the PSC and selection by departmental channels makes the process vulnerable to extraneous pressure. Local bodies such as municipal corporations and various functional agencies subject to government funding or control, can make their own arrangements for recruitment or be staffed by persons deputed from the central or state government. However, the pattern varies greatly among individual states.

### Suggestions for Reform

A committee appointed by the central government in 1998 made a number of significant recommendations relating to recruitment practices. Government has taken action on most of the expert committee's recommendations, including the issue of orders on uniform classification of posts, greater delegation to departments and the restructuring of the Central Secretariat Service and greater opportunities for employees for self-improvement.

The nodal role of the DOPT is considered critical. Government has advised the departments to revise and update recruitment rules for simplification and relevance to changing work norms and technology. This would also reduce the incidence of service litigation. It is proposed to phase out the lowest clerical levels and commence recruitment from computer-literate assistants. The DOPT is assisting other ministries to enhance their competence progressively as a step to granting greater autonomy in personnel matters. A number of scientific ministries, Railways and Posts enjoy considerable autonomy for recruiting scientific and other personnel.

## 3.3 Senior Executive Services

### *Structure*

India is unique in having some of the most important executive services in common between the federal and state governments. Two All India Services, namely the Indian Civil Service and the Imperial Police Service, existed even before independence. These services were continued under a constitutional provision and a central Act with the names Indian Administrative Service and Indian Police Service. This political decision stemmed from a recognition that these services were needed to maintain the strength and unity of the country, to provide a minimum and uniform standard of administration throughout the country, to provide competent government personnel for the emerging tasks of development and security, and to facilitate liaison between the central and state governments. The Constitution contained an enabling provision for the creation of additional services, and so far the Indian Forest Service has been created. The constitutional scheme has attracted the best talents in the country to join the AIS. Over 200,000 applicants compete for entry into these services each year.

The approach of the government was to fix the strength of state cadres of the AIS to: (a) provide for the presence of officers at different levels of responsibility in the states; (b) draw a certain number of officers to hold positions ranging from deputy secretary to secretary in the central government; and (c) spare officers for secondment to central organisations and non-government agencies. This arrangement enabled the administrative machinery at the centre to keep in touch with the realities on the ground in the states, while it helped the state administration to acquire a broader outlook and exposure and provide them with the best possible talent for filling senior positions. An additional consideration was to ensure that political considerations, both in recruitment and in discipline and control, were reduced to a minimum.

> ***Box 3.3*** **Senior Executive Services**
>
> **The Constitution envisages the establishment of All India Services by an Act of Parliament. There are three All India Services, whose members are recruited by the Union Public Service Commission, with a provision for posting in the central government and designated state cadres. These are the Indian Administrative Service, the Indian Police Service and Indian Forest Service. The AIS and important central services such as the foreign service, audit and accounts, central revenues and the higher levels of central secretariat services, railways and engineering constitute the senior executive services of administration. There are about 70,000 officers in these services.**

### *The IAS*

There is joint control over the officers of AIS by the state and central government, with the concerned central ministries having the final word in disciplinary matters, emoluments and promotion. This provides a measure of objective control, which enables officers to withstand local influence and provide independent advice. The evolution of the Indian democratic polity with different political parties in power in the central and state governments, and consequent problems faced by AIS officers during the transition to alternate political regimes, have validated this constitutional scheme.

All three All India Services consist of state and union territory cadres and the members start their service in different field posts in state government. The strength of the IAS is just under 5,000. The cadres of the IAS are composed of those selected by direct entry as well as by induction of officers of the state services to the extent of one-third the state cadre strength. Members of the UPSC preside over the committees for promotion to the AIS from state services and to a number of higher posts. The number of direct recruits to the IAS has steadily fallen over the years from about 160 in the 1960s to 59 in 2002. This reduction is designed to deal with over-expansion of the service and to ensure a more compact service.

After the directly recruited candidates are selected by the UPSC for the AIS, they are assigned to different state cadres in a transparent random process in order to ensure the representation of officers coming from regions in each state. The officers are on probation for two years. The details of the training programme for IAS officers are described in a later section.

After serving in a succession of field posts and as district collectors/ magistrates/chief executives of district development councils for the first 10–12 years, officers generally serve either in the state or state-controlled organisations or proceed to the central government under the tenure system of deputation. The management of the IAS is designed to expose young professionals to a tremendous variety of development opportunities and offers scope for innovation and the acquisition of new skills.

The IAS officers' intimate knowledge of field conditions enables them to provide sound advice to state and central departments. The officers are empanelled successively in panels of joint secretary and above according to merit and this leads to posting in different central ministries until they retire or are repatriated to state government. Some officers are selected for foreign assignment or for posting in public sector organisations. There is a calendar of training programmes within India and opportunities for training in foreign institutions with government funding. Officers can specialise in chosen fields with paid study leave of up to three years or work with accredited voluntary agencies.

The members of the IPS and IFS either work in the states in the field or at headquarters, or are posted mainly to organisations and departments in central government involving their specialised functions, such as central police and intelligence organisations, paramilitary forces, forests and environment. Any discussion of state administration should note the differences between the AIS and state cadres in respect of independence and liability to political control.

### *Organised Central Services and Central Staffing Scheme*

The officers of the IAS and central services are similar in all respects except two features. The officers of central services, whether technical or non-technical, are confined to a single department while the IAS officers can be posted to any department. Barring the officers of the

Foreign Service, members of other services are able to serve in other ministries only by virtue of the central staffing scheme. Secondly, the officers of IAS have the experience of serving in different tiers of state administration and in central organisations, while the officers of central services move within their own hierarchy.

The central secretariat service is one of the oldest organised services, and provides the staff for most ministries at the grade of under secretary and below, besides occupying many higher positions under the central staffing scheme. There is no tenure rule for these officers. Government has recently undertaken a major restructuring of this service with due regard to the need for officer-oriented organisations and the need for multi-skilled staff at the entry level.

For the three All India Services and 66 organised services in Groups A and B, entry is by direct recruitment and entry into all higher levels is by promotion and selection. Recruitment for the AIS, Groups A and B services and technical jobs such as doctors, telecom engineers and geologists, whether through direct recruitment or selection, generally takes place under the supervision of the UPSC.

The central staffing scheme for preparing panels of officers from the AIS and different central services (except the Indian Foreign Service) is operated by the DOPT through the Civil Services Board, which is headed by the Cabinet Secretary. The posts include board level appointments to central public sector undertakings and appointments of joint secretaries, directors and deputy secretaries in the ministries and departments. The proposals require the approval of the Appointments Committee of the Cabinet, headed by the Prime Minister. The DOPT also hosts the central establishment board for the posts of and above under secretary up to joint secretary in consultation with individual ministries. The Foreign Service Board, Railway Board and the Defence Services Selection Board deal with the empanelment and appointment of officers in their respective services.

The Cabinet Secretariat prepares the panels for appointment as secretaries and additional secretaries with the approval of the ACC. Officers on the panel are assigned to various ministries and positions in central government. There were 128 officers working at secretary level, 109 at the level of additional secretary and 446 at the level of joint secretary at the end of 2002.

### *Lateral Entry and Mobility*

The Rules for AIS, and many central services do not envisage lateral recruitment at levels higher than the entry post or one level above. Apart from provisions for deputation of officers to state enterprises and external aid agencies, there are provisions in the rules of AIS and a number of state services to permit the deputation of senior officials to work in private sector or NGOs subject to avoidance of conflict of interest. There is an increasing movement of central and state officers to reputed voluntary agencies because of the attraction of working on burning social issues. An earlier section has referred to the progressive provisions in some state governments.

### *Challenges before the AIS and Central Services*

Otherwise known as the 'steel frame', the IAS officers increasingly represent the entire spectrum of population and educational disciplines. Among the challenges for the IAS and IPS are the frequent transfers disrupting the tenor of administration and efficiency and morale of officers, especially in the states. Central control over AIS continues to be a thorny issue in centre-state relations especially with diverse political parties controlling governments in the centre and states. The technical services and outside experts fault the IAS for their generalist orientation in contrast to the need for specialised skills.

The system of performance assessment, with some exceptions as in Railways and foreign service, has not been sufficiently participatory and transparent and does not assist in performance improvement or career planning (Box 3.4). Different central services operate in vertical silos and are jealous about influx from other services. Individual ministries have not fully explored the scope for cadre rationalisation and the consolidation of cadres with similar functions such as audit, accounts and engineering.

Central government has been advising the state governments to assure minimum tenure to officers of the AIS in different field and senior management positions, and has mooted amendments to the AIS Rules to give legal effect to institutional arrangement similar to civil service boards. The other challenge common to all levels of administration is the restoration of ethical standards. Government is amending the Code of Conduct to enable greater transparency, while prosecuting all cases of corrupt behaviour.

**Box 3.4 Performance Assessment and Career Development of the AIS and Central Services**

**The recommendations of the Surendranath Committee Report on performance assessment and career development of AIS officers include the organisation of functional streams for specialisation and preparing officers for assuming higher positions through focused training on the model of the Canadian programme. Eleven domains have been selected for assignment streaming for officers under the central staffing scheme. The output of the empanelment process would be a list of officers found suitable for selection to specific positions under the Central Staffing Scheme, together with their respective domain assignments. All senior executive services would specify career-training programmes, which would be mandatory for promotion to different levels. This would be supplemented by opportunities for self-development through foreign training programmes and sabbatical leave. Government is examining the report.**

## 3.4 Pay and Benefits Policy

Pay, allowances and various benefits are periodically determined by the Government on the basis of the recommendations of pay commissions (usually appointed every ten years), followed by negotiation with recognised employee unions. The last pay commission, the fifth, submitted its report in 1997. Besides the question of government resources, the principles for fixing pay are inclusiveness, comprehensiveness, model employer, pay in the private sector and adequacy. The number of payscales has been progressively reduced over the years and the salary for the entire civil service is regulated now with reference to 35 payscales. The increments range from 1.64 to 3.44 per cent of the minimum of the scale. The Pay Commission establishes the equivalence of different positions in various services and fits them into each scale. The effort has also been to delink pay from position in the hierarchy. There are problems of vertical and horizontal relativity and problems in fitting posts of varying qualifications and functions in different departments into one or other payscale.

The decision on the recommendations of the Pay Commission is taken on the basis of consultation with recognised staff unions. There is a provision for committees to resolve anomalies. There is also provision for the appointment of an independent arbitrator to make the final decision on differences relating to pay, allowances and leave, subject only to the authority of Parliament.

Following the report of the FCPC, the compression or disparity ratio between the maximum and minimum pay and dearness allowance is around 11.76 with reference to maximum monthly pay of Rs. 30,000. This is in line with international trends and the ratio will be maintained by the dispensation of 100 per cent neutralisation for inflation for serving and retired employees. The ratio ranges from 7 to 12 in state governments.

Dearness allowance (DA) is linked to the consumer price index and is intended to neutralise the erosion of wages by inflation. A major decision in 1997 was to agree to 100 per cent neutralisation of inflation for serving employees and pensioners through increases in dearness allowances twice a year. After DA crosses 50 per cent of basic pay, government may decide to merge pay and DA.

Apart from basic pay and DA, major allowances and benefits include house rent and city compensatory allowance, hardship allowance for those working in difficult areas, non-practising allowance for doctors, transport and travel allowance, leave travel concession, subsidised accommodation, medical facilities, group insurance, low interest loans for housing and conveyance and a variety of allowances in individual departments. There are special allowances for people working in difficult areas, project allowances, reimbursement of tuition fees in certain circumstances and overtime allowance. Productivity-linked bonuses are paid to employees in departmental enterprises such as Railways and Posts, while regular employees up to a certain salary level are paid an *ex gratia* amount on the basis of a formula.

State governments have followed the example of central government in fixing the pay scales, allowances and termination benefits of their own employees.

### *Terminal Benefits and Pensions*

The retirement age for central government employees is 60, while it ranges from 55 to 60 in the states. As a measure to encourage the exit of personnel, all regular employees have the option of retiring after an eligible service of 20 years and they are provided with a five-year benefit in calculating pension and gratuity. A more attractive package with an *ex gratia* payment is available to encourage the voluntary exit of surplus central staff.

### *Box 3.5* Terminal Benefits for Employees

**Terminal benefits include pension, gratuity, encashment of accumulated leave up to 240 days, balance in contributory provident fund and group insurance. Employees are eligible for a pension after seven years of eligible service and are denied pension in case of resignation. The basis of the pension is 50 per cent of the average basic pay for the last ten months of service (subject to a maximum of Rs. 15,000), subject to a reckonable service of 33 years and a pro rata reduction for lesser years of service at the time of retirement. Dearness allowance is payable on pension similar to that for serving employees. The employees can commute up to 40 per cent of the pension. Gratuity is calculated at the rate of 0.25 per cent of basic pay and dearness allowance for every six months of eligible service subject to a maximum of Rs. 25,0000. Family pension up to a maximum of 30 per cent of basic pay is paid to the spouse of deceased employees. The Indian government follows the defined benefit principle for pension on a pay-as-you-go basis, but the Government has recently announced a major decision to move to a defined contribution system for persons entering government service from January 2004.**

Employees contribute to a general provident fund (GPF) with no matching contribution by government. Loans can be taken from the accumulated balance for specified purposes and the balance can be withdrawn by the employee at the time of retirement.

The Department of Pensions and Pensioners Welfare is the nodal department for all matters relating to pensions and the welfare of pensioners. Many reforms have been introduced to improve the system for sanction and disbursement of pension, such as centralised monitoring, computerisation and monthly payment of pension and periodical increases in DA through the branches of nationalised banks in the place of residence of the pensioner. A standing committee of representatives of pensioners interacts regularly with government on pensioner grievance and welfare.

#### *Challenges*

Central government now recognises the cascading effect of its liberal policies on pay and allowances and hopes to develop an All India approach for containing wage costs. The salary bills of central and state government employees together have reached nearly half the revenue receipts. Equally problematic has been the tremendous increase in pension expenditure, but this could come down for future employees with the decision on contributory pension. As important as the basic pay in the growth of expenditure are the dearness allowance and other allowances paid to employees. Beyond the fiscal burden and the affordability of the civil service, these high salary awards are questionable on equity grounds since the ratio of the average central government wage to per capita GDP is high.

While the time for the appointment of the next Pay Commission is due, government appears to be reviewing various options in the light of international practices. Greater consultation with state governments on granting future benefits is envisaged because of the demand of state employees for parity with central pay scales and the consequent impact on state finances.

## 3.5 Establishment Control and Institutional Capacity

### *Role of the DOPT*

The Ministry of Personnel, Public Grievances and Pensions is the co-ordinating agency in the central government in personnel matters, especially recruitment, training, career development, staff welfare, terminal benefits, public grievances and administrative reforms. The Ministry is under a single permanent secretary but consists of the Department of Personnel and Training, the Department of Administrative Reforms and Public Grievances and the Department of Pensions and Pensioner Welfare. The DOPT is the nodal department for personnel management as originally conceived by the Administrative Reforms Commission.

At a more immediate level, the DOPT has the direct responsibility of being the cadre-controlling authority for the Indian Administrative Service and the Central Secretariat Service. The Department also operates the Central Staffing Scheme and deals with senior appointments to public sector boards and management, as mentioned above. It deals with the assignment of Indian experts to various developing countries. It administers the national training policy and assists state governments in various ways to train their personnel.

The DOPT also controls a number of statutory organisations and other agencies. These include recruitment agencies, namely the Union Public Service Commission, the Staff Selection Commission and the Public Enterprises Selection Board; vigilance bodies, namely the Central Vigilance Commissioner and chief vigilance officers; training organisations such as the Lal Bahadur Shastri National Academy of Administration (LBSNAA) and Institute of Secretariat Training and Management (ISTM); and the quasi-judicial body for service matters, the Central Administrative Tribunal.

The responsibility for establishment control is divided between the Department of Expenditure in the Ministry of Finance and the Ministry of Personnel, Pensions and Public Grievances, especially the Department of Personnel and Training. The DOPT is frequently called upon by various ministries and departments to give its opinion on complex, difficult and sensitive issues.

The UPSC plays no direct role in personnel management. The Department of Expenditure and the DOPT jointly decide issues relating to pay and allowances and terminal benefits and matters arising out of the recommendations of pay commissions. Both departments jointly monitor the implementation of orders relating to preparation and enforcement of recruitment plans by departments, abolition of vacant posts and the redeployment of surplus staff. Both are involved in negotiations with the unions on staff and benefits. In its larger nodal role, the Personnel Ministry acts as the formulator of policy and as the watchdog of the government, ensuring that certain accepted standards and norms, including reservation of posts and vigilance, are followed by all ministries and departments in recruitment, regulation of service conditions and labour relations.

### *Challenges: Centralisation versus Autonomy and Building Capacity*

In practice, control over central government staff is fragmented among ministries, which deal with management of cadres other than the IAS. Just four Ministries, Railways, Defence, Home and Posts (the number was higher before the corporatisation of telecommunications) are responsible for about 86 per cent of government staff.

The management of the Central Secretariat Service has been decentralised, with the ministries being responsible for secretariat staff up to the level of section officers subject to guidelines issued by the

DOPT. Substantial numbers of Group D staff are under the direct control of ministries and their agencies though subject to economy instructions and guidelines of the DOPT and Ministry of Finance. The personnel database also tends to be fragmented and this affects the tracking of civil service numbers continuously in the Ministries of Finance and Personnel except in the case of cadres controlled by them.

It was only after the acceptance of the report of the Expenditure Reforms Commission that government moved towards a collegial approach to establishment control. As discussed in another section, the reviews of staff levels by department level screening committees are predicated on functional reviews and flexibility in deciding on reductions in workforce and redeployment within global staff reduction targets. Other problems of establishment control are also being addressed, such as the revision and updating of recruitment rules with the support of the DOPT and expert committees.

It is not evident that India is in a position to move away from centralised establishment control towards totally decentralised systems such those which operate in New Zealand or the running cost approach to departmental autonomy as in the UK. It is true that large departments like Railways are already implementing decentralised systems of the type advocated in other Commonwealth countries. At the same time, most ministries are not adequately equipped with well-resourced HRM divisions and may not be able to cope with total autonomy. The current problem may in fact be ineffectively enforced central control, partly due to lack of adequate capacity and inadequate management information system in the Ministries of Finance and Personnel.

The proliferation of service cadres and their increasing overlap must be seen in the context of the historical context of the emergence and fragmentation of different departments over time. It has given rise to serious issues of unequal service conditions and prospects among employees performing similar functions in different service cadres. Urgent attention is needed to remedy these deficiencies before moving further towards departmental autonomy.

It is difficult to escape the impression that personnel management in most states enjoys low priority, and is fragmented and reactive. Personnel departments tend to concentrate on postings, promotions, transfers and routine service matters, to the neglect of larger and long-term considerations of human resource management. Recent reforms in some states seek to ensure that the personnel department fully undertakes its currently defined responsibilities as a co-ordinating and integrating agency for the management of government personnel.

An important problem confronting many states and central ministries is the court-mandated absorption of temporary and daily wage staff. Court decisions mandating the absorption of labour declared surplus or retrenched have reflected broader societal expectations that the government should be the model employer for the country. Recent court rulings, however, suggest a gradual shift in opinion on these cases and courts have ruled that the question of downsizing or rightsizing was a policy matter and that the making of policy was outside the purview of the courts except to the extent of observance of fair process.

Efforts to upgrade HRM capacity and information base in the personnel department are in progress in central and state governments. The first step for central and state personnel departments is to build the capacity of cadre-controlling authorities on a phased basis, using information gathered from the inventory of service cadres and rules. Government is establishing mechanisms to ensure that the strength of service cadres is reviewed regularly and aligned with functional requirements. Andhra Pradesh state has set up strategy and performance innovation units in key departments, which will be provided with outside consultant support for HRM and action plans.

The Finance Department has played the lead role in personnel matters in central and state governments as a means of controlling salary costs and it has functioned as a gatekeeper on approvals to create new posts and fill vacant ones. It is now realised that, while this objective is important for fiscally strained governments, a well-equipped personnel department needs to take charge of the HRM function and work closely with the Finance Department.

## 3.6 Human Resource Information System and Planning

Lack of good personnel management information has limited the ability of central and state governments to administer their public services effectively and efficiently, or to maintain adequate control over the growth and composition of the entire civil service establishment.

Information on civil service personnel in central government is fragmented across organised services and clusters of posts in isolated cadres. Only large and established ministries like Railways maintain computerised databases of personnel at headquarters and divisional level for the purpose of personnel management and treasury control. A centralised and constantly updated database on employees and emoluments is yet to be constructed by the Ministry of Personnel or Finance, let alone developed as a HRM tool. The central budget relies mainly on the figures compiled by the Pay Research Unit on central employees which are published every year. Manpower estimates are based on attrition and projections of staff accretions are related to the expansion or addition of schemes.

The DOPT, Home Ministry and Revenue Department have built a dynamic executive information system for IAS, IPS and Revenue officers. The Revenue Department's website helps an officer to build and maintain his service profile throughout his or her service career. The officer can secure personal data through a password much in the manner of systems devised in Andhra Pradesh's *Smartgov* system. The officer is equipped to continuously update his or her data in the course of different stages of their career and training.

### *Box 3.6* Human Resource Information System in States

**Andhra Pradesh has completed a comprehensive civil service census and placed the information on its website. Uttar Pradesh is in the process of establishing a computerised personnel management information system (called DEMIST) of all personnel employed by the government, including pensioners and workers on daily wage. The systems designed by Uttar Pradesh and Andhra Pradesh will address the needs for human resource management, monitoring transfers and reviewing the progress of rightsizing strategies. These information systems will also be linked with integrated payroll and accounting systems and measures for financial control over unauthorised creation of posts. In the *Smartgov* system for the Secretariat, Andhra Pradesh employees will have access to all non-confidential aspects of information relating to past and present service, pay and allowances, provident fund, leave, official circulars and status of applications.**

The Surendranath Committee on Performance Appraisal has proposed a re-designation of the personal dossier of each senior officer in order to mesh with the revised format for appraisal. The personnel dossier could then become a comprehensive source of information about an officer for different personnel actions such as confirmation, promotion to a higher grade, empanelment, selection to particular positions and retirement from service. The dossier would include information on performance in a given position or grade, professional qualification, academic and research output, work experience, exceptional accomplishments and general reputation.

### *Staff Norms*

Efforts at staff rationalisation in the 1960s focused on the establishment of O&M cells and administrative reform units in central ministries to carry out detailed studies and to suggest improvement in the administrative structure and methods of work under the supervision of the Department of Administrative Reforms.

The Staff Inspection Unit (SIU) was set up in 1964 under the Ministry of Finance. The object was to effect economies in manpower consistent with administrative efficiency and evolve performance standards and work norms in government offices and institutions which were wholly or substantially dependent on government grants. Its officers also serve as core members on the committees appointed to scrutinise the manpower requirements of scientific organisations.

The productivity of many posts in central and state government cannot be observed or related to compensation on the basis of scientific norms. The SIU's exercises were complemented by cadre reviews undertaken by the Department of Personnel and work studies of individual departments. The SIU developed norms for staffing in respect of common jobs and functions in different government organisations based on time and motion studies. Until 1998, the SIU carried out studies for about 658,000 posts, declared about 98,000 posts as surplus and rejected proposals for a similar number. Major ministries like Railways and Telecommunications choose to operate their own norms. The studies complemented efforts by the Finance Ministry and Planning Commission to identify and weed out redundant schemes in various central organisations and devolve central schemes to states as part of a planning and annual budget exercise. It is proposed to rationalise the existing methodology of cadre reviews and the SIU.

The creation of divisions in health, education and engineering establishments in central government is based on norms of expenditure or coverage of target group or geographic area and these norms are regularly revised on the basis of the changing nature of current functions or the value of money.

The approach of state governments to staff rationalisation has been less systematic and there are no dedicated units for the exercise. Central norms have guided state departments such as those for irrigation, public works and health. Andhra Pradesh set up a staff review committee in 1994 following directions of the Supreme Court and undertook a detailed review of norms for creating field units and the creation of posts in 40 departments. Andhra Pradesh and other states are undertaking exercises for staff review in engineering and secretariat establishments in the light of recent developments in technology, scope for modernisation, efforts for outsourcing and devolution. A number of state finance commissions have worked out the norms for local services and staff in the course of making recommendations on the functions and devolution of funds for elected local bodies. The agenda for civil service reform in some states seeks to increase the proportion of front-line employees such as teachers and health personnel, while reducing unnecessary support staff.

## 3.7 Performance Appraisal

### *The Present System*

Because of its impact on salary and career prospects, the framework for performance appraisal has important consequences for the motivation of employees, and thus for efficient and improved performance. Although supervisors have the opportunity for continuous feedback from employees and for guidance, annual confidential reports (ACRs) are the principal means of periodic formal appraisal. Due to historical factors underlying the evolution of the confidential rolls, ACRs have been considered to be identical with performance assessment despite the incongruity of the term.

The system of writing ACRs has three principal objectives. One is the organisational objective of ensuring the most effective contribution of each employee to the goals of the department and government. Second is the improvement in performance of the person reported upon in his or her present job. The third is to assess the employee's potential and prepare him or her through suitable feedback, guidance and training for further advancement. ACRs are also meant to be used in connection with the personnel functions of training and human resource development, promotion and confirmation of employees, award of increments and assured career progression, and decisions on continuing in service after the stipulated years of service have been served.

The ACR format is different for the AIS and central services. Technical ministries like Railways and scientific departments prescribe special formats to suit the requirements of individual functions in the department. ACRs are usually in separate formats for the senior executives, supervisors and Group C personnel. ACR formats have been revised a number of times in central and state governments, often on the recommendation of expert committees. The format for AIS officers is prescribed by the central Department of Personnel and is quite elaborate. Since 1986, most ministries have incorporated a section for self-appraisal by the employee, which indicates the nature of functions and assigned targets of performance. This is expected to assist the reporting officer in recording comments.

The reports are expected to be written after the end of the financial year in April. Guidelines have been issued to the reporting officers on rating the employees under different headings, and then giving an overall grading ranging from outstanding to very good, good, average and below average. There are columns for the employee's state of health and integrity. At the middle and senior levels, there are columns for suggestions for training. The critical columns relate to fitness for promotion or continuance in the present post, and a confidential assessment of the employee's integrity. In most states, the formats are uniform for all employees regardless of the nature of their function or the nature of their assignment in the secretariat or autonomous enterprise or the district. Besides the section on self-assessment, the forms provide a supplementary sheet to allow for the recording of remarks on technical performance in the case of the Departments of Engineering, Health, Accounts and Technology. Most states do not insist on the writing of ACRs for Group D staff. In some states, such as Andhra Pradesh and Tamil Nadu, ACRs are not recorded for non-gazetted employees and this makes assessment of performance difficult. Discussions between the evaluator and employee being evaluated are infrequent. Only adverse remarks are communicated and the employee is entitled to submit a representation to get the remarks expunged.

The departmental rules prescribe the reporting and reviewing officer and the accepting authority for each level of government servant. The grading and remarks of the reporting officer are reviewed by the superior officer and then forwarded with or without changes to the accepting authority. While the process is generally secretive, the armed forces and some states practise openness in varying degrees consistent with the international trend. Some public sector enterprises have also introduced participatory appraisal of officers. For AIS officers, ACRs are maintained by the DOPT, while other departments maintain ACRs for cadres controlled by them.

### *Deficiencies of the Present System*

In the opinion of a number of expert committees, the non-transparent, subjective and unilateral character of the ACR in central and state governments has reduced its utility for public agencies. They have pointed out the deficiencies of the ACR system in practice, including:

- Use of uniform and cumbersome formats, without regard to the different types of functions and work performed in different departments;
- The high level of subjectivity, and the scope for bias and victimisation on the part of reporting and reviewing officers;
- Arbitrary grading of employees, unrelated to actual performance, and the tendency to grade most employees very high to avoid incurring the displeasure of subordinates;
- Failure to provide for the evaluation of traits relevant to the assessment of front-line employees and citizen orientation;
- The non-participatory character of the review and the failure to agree on targets at the beginning of the year;
- Problems of multiple reporting by officers and overload on heads of departments; and
- Limited utility in identifying employees who deserve to be encouraged or poor performers who need to be watched, and in developing the employees' potential.

In many states, the ACR process has been allowed to atrophy because – beyond the threat of an adverse entry – it was not viewed as important in determining career progression. The promotion exercise is often reduced to one of preparing the panel purely on the basis of seniority or relative shades of very good grades. ACRs are not available in time for consideration by Departmental Promotion Committees (DPCs) and employees suffer from delays in writing ACRs. The system as a whole suffers from inadequate monitoring of the quality and timeliness of performance assessment at the level of secretaries or heads of departments in central government and their counterparts in the states.

The cumulative effect of these deficiencies has been the gradual erosion of the credibility of ACRs as a fair and objective means of testing employee performance. Staff unions have been demanding the abolition of ACRs on the grounds of their ineffectiveness and the scope for their use as an instrument of vicitimisation.

At the same time, the ACR continues to be a tool for deciding the advancement and career development of employees. Hence, the employee's immediate loyalty is to the person reporting or reviewing the ACR, and the authorities involved in deciding matters of seniority and selection for higher posts. This distorts accountability of front-line staff and managers in service delivery.

### *Approach to Reform*

It is generally agreed that serious efforts to reform the system of performance assessment are urgently needed. The suggestions from experts and employee unions involve removing the secrecy surrounding the process and making the review participatory on the basis of agreed goals and measures. Some progressive states envisage that the ACR process requires regular year-end feedback sessions between supervisory and subordinate staff and that outcome-based performance evaluation systems should be devised and put in place in all the departments. Online performance indicators, as in Andhra Pradesh, are expected to provide a more objective and acceptable basis for assessing performance even in the case of non-gazetted officials.

At the same time, process reforms are envisaged to reduce the responsibility for initiating ACRs to manageable levels for each supervisor and head of department, to impose strict time limits for the submission of ACRs after the end of the financial year, and take action against reporting officers for unwarranted delays. A number of state departments are devising their own ACR formats, suited to the functional needs of different jobs, and the format is also being simplified. Arrangements for monitoring the entire process of appraisal will be improved with computerised systems, as has already undertaken by some ministries and states. A number of ministries are considering the adoption of a ten-point scale for executive cadres on the lines of that in place in the armed forces instead of grading.

### *Performance Assessment for AIS Officers*

While the broad structure of the ACR *pro forma* is the same for the IPS and IFS as for the IAS, there are differences with regard to the specific attributes evaluated, given the differences in the nature of the work entrusted to the IPS and IFS in relation compared with the IAS. The recommendations of the 2003 Surendranath Committee on Performance Appraisal provide major directions of reform for performance appraisal, placement and career advancement of the AIS. Based on the report of Committee on Performance Assessment in 2003, government proposes to amend the ACR format for the AIS to allow for the preparation of an agreed work plan at the beginning of the year, more effective and compact assessment of traits, disclosure of the contents of the assessment and an opportunity to make representations to a review board. Government is also considering an institutionalised system of an Eminent Persons Group (EPG) for a 360 degree assessment of the officer, which can guide the government in decisions relating to special assignments or weeding out inefficient staff. It is also proposed to define the objectives of the assessment with clear links to HRM functions.

### *Screening Performance and Dealing with Poor Performers*

Once a person enters government service, screening of performance can take place at different levels for different groups and cadres: at the stage of confirmation after probation, conversion of temporary into permanent status, lateral entry of serving employees into higher posts, selection for prized assignments and study fellowships. Some state governments have enforced efficiency bars for movements into higher payscales.

The rule on compulsory or premature retirement is based on the Doctrine of Pleasure under Article 310 of the Constitution. Public interest rather than rightsizing underlies the operation of the rule. The termination of service following the order of compulsory retirement should be distinguished from the retrenchment of redundant staff following an organisational review or the punishment of removal following disciplinary proceedings. The decision would be based on a review of his or her past performance by an appropriate authority after the completion of the stipulated qualifying period (ranging from 20 to 25 years of regular service), or after attaining 50 years based on a review of ACRs and other evidence of performance and integrity. The Indian Defence Forces (IDF) follow the principle of easing out officers who fail to make the grade for promotion to higher levels, on the principle of 'up or out'.

Having studied the reasons for infrequent recourse to the provision, government proposes to enforce the existing rule for premature retirement more rigorously by strengthening the as performance assessment system and by addressing legal infirmities in the procedure. The in objective of weeding out the dead wood would be placed in the broader context of improving HRM and performance evaluation practices.

The Karnataka Government is considering amending the rules to require all employees to take an efficiency bar test at the end of 15 years of service and again after 25 years. The test would be objective, with department-specific papers on service rules and technical knowledge, and would be conducted by the Public Service Commission. Any government employees who failed to secure the prescribed minimum marks would be compulsorily retired.

## 3.8 Transfers and Placement Transfer Guidelines

Transfer is a fact of administrative life. The central and state service rules provide that a member of a service or class of service may be required to serve in any post falling under the remit of such a service for which he or she is qualified. Transfer could be to another workstation in an equivalent post or to another category with the same payscale or within a defined territory such as a district for education and health staff. It could involve deputation to a public undertaking. Rules and executive instructions specify the appropriate authority for transferring personnel at various levels and this power can extend to local bodies as well.

### *Box 3.7* Transfer Policy of the Department of Revenue and other Central Departments

In an effort to make the process of transfer of its officers transparent and corruption-free, the Department of Revenue in the Ministry of Finance has made it mandatory for its Group A officers to seek transfers only through a ministry website. The Department has also asked its officers to submit an executive profile detailing their career data. At the time of annual general transfer, applications for transfer by all officers of the Indian Revenue Service will be accepted only through the online system. Submission of an executive profile will be a precondition to access the online submission of the transfer application. The move is seen as the first step in the right direction to avoid unnecessary favouritism in transfers. The officers can be sure of whether their application for transfer is on record and can verify whether there are any inappropriate incidents. Apart from the benefits of transparency and the elimination of corruption in the process, the officers can also place on record their preferences and requests, which will be taken up according to merit. Other ministries and departments are expected to follow this example.

The transfer policy for the Ordnance Factories Board has four obligations: functional requirement, career development of officers through wider exposure, rotation in sensitive posts and accommodation of requests on compassionate grounds. The central police organisations undertake an exercise of rotation of personnel from difficult to normal areas.

The guidelines and regulations of central and state governments are widely publicised on the web and through booklets. They usually provide for:

- Specification of committees for recommending transfers of staff at different levels;
- All transfers to be effected only during a stipulated transfer period, say, April to May each year, except for transfers necessitated by promotions or retirement or disciplinary action;
- General transfer or change of post after a specified period for each employee;

- Prescription of a minimum and maximum period of stay in one post for different types of posts, having regard both to stability and avoiding scope for abuse of office;
- Policy of posting husband and wife together in the same place or nearby;
- Not posting employees to their native district except for district cadres and Group D staff;
- Special provisions in case of handicapped persons or persons on the verge of retirement;
- Transfers necessitated by the need to deploy large numbers of personnel on account of sudden contingencies or emergencies, or on time-bound projects;
- Transfers on request or on compassionate grounds.

### *Problems and Reform*

In recent times, there has been considerable concern among governments and officials about tenures of less than one year, and the effect which arbitrary transfers can have on the morale and efficiency of officials at different levels. Mass transfers of officers belonging to different services were made in some states following a change in the political complexion of the government. The non-transparency of the transfer process and inadequate machinery and information for tracking transfers at global and local level complicated efforts for reform in central and state governments.

There is growing political agreement around the operation of objective and transparent criteria for transfers and promotions. It is realised that stability of tenure of officials, who are at the cutting edge of administration in different fields, provides them with sufficient local knowledge and experience to deal with different issues and implement schemes more efficiently as administration becomes increasingly decentralised. The responsiveness and even-handed attitude of a civil servant is seen as depending to a substantial extent on the degree to which he or she does not feel threatened by the risk of premature transfer or any punishment for fair administration. Thus, the people, civil servants and the administration at large, all have a vital stake in stability of tenure.

Proposals for ensuring stable tenure have focused on insulating the process from the unwarranted influence of political and extraneous factors. The National Police Commission (and expert committees on police reform in recent years) have suggested the establishment of statutory state security commissions in each state, which would consist of independent citizens and opposition legislators, and be headed by the Chief Minister. The Security Commission would, *inter alia*, lay down policy guidelines on the preventive and service functions of police, and serve as a forum of appeal for officials aggrieved by decisions on service matters, including premature transfers.

A variant of this proposal is the scheme of independent civil service boards (CSBs) to recommend measures for personnel management, transfer and placement of officers and provide a form of appeal for officers with a genuine grievance. In respect of the central staffing scheme, the committee under the Cabinet Secretary already plays the role envisaged for CSBs. It is proposed to consult the states about amendments to the AIS Rules to set up CSBs, specify minimum tenures for AIS officers and provide opportunities for representation to officers in cases of premature transfer.

Some states are moving forward with progressive policies on transfers. Many posts are being constituted into district cadres to reduce the incidence of moving officials across large states at considerable inconvenience and cost. Maharashtra has enacted legislation to curb the arbitrary transfer of government officials in the state. The new law will fix minimum and maximum tenures of officers in districts and head offices.

Karnataka Government has created an institutional framework based on rules and reinforced by transparency and public information to regulate transfers, thus remoulding the politically driven process. It took a far-reaching step in 2000 to constitute cadre management authorities to screen and effect transfers for officials at different levels and belonging to different departments. The concerned Minister was designated the chairperson for Group A posts in the department to give the Minister a sense of involvement in rational policies. A separate committee reporting to the Chief Minister oversees transfers of officers of the AIS and the state administrative service. The government fixed a minimum tenure of three years for Group A officers, four years for Group B, five years for Group C and seven years for Group D. Premature transfers were prohibited except in specified circumstances and with the Minister's approval. Certain cadres like teachers and nurses were exempted from transfers.

Transfer is only one aspect of the issue of proper placement of officers according to their qualifications and experience. Uttar Pradesh made an effort in 2000 to develop position qualifications and classifications for over 1,800 Class I and Class II positions in order to promote greater mobility across services, facilitate greater specialisation through career planning and training, and enable more rational postings; but this was not followed up in the changed regime. The significance of the Uttar Pradesh effort was the location of transfer policy within the broader context of civil service reform and professionalisation of personnel.

The Surendranath Committee recommended a specific scheme for functional specialisation and placement of officers and for building this exercise into empanelment and training. With regard to placements in the Government of India, at the level of joint secretary and above, it is envisaged that the skills and backgrounds of officers are optimally used.

The more progressive element relates to the *counselling system* based on transparent consultation with employees in different departments and decisions on transfer related to incentives and objective criteria. The counselling approach can help to tackle non-responsive and inefficient delivery of key public services in backward areas. It can tackle the problem of absenteeism of front-line employees by linking subsequent postings to performance and by rewarding time spent in backward areas with higher scores, while reducing the scope for arbitrary and secretive transfers. The system is working well, starting with the education departments in some states. It has raised the morale and efficiency of officers while eliciting public support.

Andhra Pradesh has institutionalised counselling in the form of rules and a points system for deciding on requests for transfers, based on past performance, examination results and time spent in remote areas. The Government has set up committees to provide access to employees in field positions. Karnataka has clarified and codified the rules for prioritising requests for transfers from rural teachers and set up an electronic database of available vacancies to match transfer requests.

A reliable database on transfers is essential to verify whether measures to curb transfers are having an impact, to enable the political leadership to claim credit if there is a positive impact, and to establish a better understanding of the problem across departments. Karnataka has developed a comprehensive database, available on its website, to track transfers over time for the last six years. It includes data on aggregate transfers, transfers by department, reasons for transfer and transfers by cadre for Group A posts. It is the first time that a state government has created a publicly accessible and continually updated database to monitor transfers over time. The introduction of transparency in the transfer process will help to reduce the element of secrecy shrouding the process, generate public pressure to reduce the abuses and extend support to change agents within the government to initiate reforms.

## 3.9 Promotion and Performance Incentives

### *Promotion Policies*

The problem of ensuring adequate career progression of employees is perennial for all departments. Reasonable promotion opportunities ranging from two to four in an officer's career have been generally accepted as a norm. In any service or cadre, different proportions of posts will be filled by direct recruitment, departmental promotion, promotion either by selection or by non-selection, transfer or deputation. The persons recruited through the various methods will have different promotion prospects depending on vacant posts, seniority and merit.

To deal with the problem of stagnation and inadequate promotion opportunities, different departments undertake cadre reviews at regular intervals to identify posts and grades that can be upgraded, and redundant posts that can be abolished consistent with functional requirements and improved efficiency of the organisation. Government recently took a decision on the restructuring of the CSS on the basis of the recommendation of a committee. Dissatisfaction with cadre reviews has led to the demand of central service employees for time-bound promotion.

Different criteria are adopted for promotion of employees to higher posts depending on the group, such as seniority and fitness, seniority and merit, and selection by merit depending on the post and the function. Promotion criteria are different for selection and non-selection posts. In non-selection posts, promotion occurs according to seniority subject to rejection of unfit employees or persons with a bad vigilance record. In the case of selection posts, the department promotion committee grades officers as 'fit' or 'unfit' based on the benchmark. For higher posts (less than 5 per cent of the total number of posts), there is a higher benchmark of 'very good', but persons with grades higher than the benchmark cannot overtake others in the seniority list. The limited departmental competitive examination for promotion to certain posts such as section officer is based on the principle of faster promotion for more competent employees.

Reservation in cases of promotion by non-selection is available to members of SC and ST in all the groups of services at the rate of 15 per cent and 7.5 per cent respectively. In case of promotion by selection method, reservation for SC and ST is available up to the lowest rung of Group A at the same percentages. There is no reservation for OBC in promotion.

Government seeks to ensure the merit principle through the preparation of panels by departmental promotion committees (DPCs), which are constituted by individual departments for officials from Groups A, B and C. The committees are headed by officers of appropriate status, starting from the chief secretary down to the head of department and district officers. Detailed guidelines govern the procedure to be followed by these committees, such as the zone of promotion, seniority lists, assessment of ACRs, reservation policy, preparation of evaluation sheets in the order of seniority and consideration of reports of integrity and disciplinary proceedings. The panel is finalised on the basis of consideration of these factors, but actual promotion of persons in the panel is subject to vacancies. The state governments follow a similar policy. There is no uniform policy among departments on transparency of proceedings of the DPCs.

### *Promotion in the Senior Executive Service*

The formal channel of promotions for all the All India Services and other Group A services is their respective state/departmental cadre. In respect of the All India Services, executive instructions for such promotions are issued by the respective administrative ministries of the Government of India, namely the DOPT for the IAS, the Home Ministry for the IPS and the Ministry of Environment and Forests for the IFOS. Cabinet Secretary and state chief secretaries are appointed by a process of selection according to merit. In respect of the AIS, the requirement of consultation with the UPSC has been dispensed with. However, in the case of other Group A Services (except for the Indian Foreign Service), the Departmental Promotion Committees are chaired by a member of the UPSC. Placements of officers of the All-India Services as well as for other Group A Services under the Central Staffing Scheme involves two stages, empanelment and selection for particular positions.

Empanelment is the process of drawing up a shortlist of officers from the All-India Services and other Group A Services for possible selection to positions under the Central Staffing Scheme. This exercise is normally conducted annually, considering officers with the same year of allotment together. Empanelment relates strictly to suitability for holding posts under the central government. It is not a substantive promotion to a higher grade.

For the posts of additional secretary and secretary in central government, empanelment is based on the recommendations of a four-member committee consisting of the Cabinet Secretary, the Principal Secretary to the Prime Minister, the Home Secretary and Secretary to the Department of Personnel. The panel is then submitted for approval of the ACC. Inclusion in the panel is through a process of strict selection and evaluation of such qualities as merit, competence, leadership and a flair for participation in the policy-making process. The state governments issue executive instructions for promotion to the super-time (joint secretary level) and higher levels in government. The Screening Committee consists of the Chief Secretary as Chairman and two other officers working at the grade of Principal Secretary in the state government concerned as members.

### *Reforming the System*

There is some frustration with the operation of current guidelines for promotion in central and state services. Disparities in recruitment rules in ministries lead to varying promotion prospects for similarly qualified persons in different services, while many cadres experience stagnation. Promotions are held up by delays in the constitution of DPCs and in the preparation of panels, and by problems with seniority lists and litigation. Ad hoc promotions to posts to cope with delays in the finalisation of panels or delays in direct recruitment create additional problems of regularisation and litigation by disgruntled employees.

**_Box 3.8_ The Assured Career Progression Scheme**

**The assured career progression (ACP) scheme installed in 1998 is viewed as a safety net to deal with the problem of genuine stagnation and hardship faced by employees due to lack of adequate avenues for promotion. It is available to regular employees, other than those in Group A, in the form of two financial upgrades on completion of 12 and 24 years service. Introduction of the ACP scheme, however, in no case affects the normal (regular) promotional avenues available on the basis of vacancies and ACP is not construed as regular promotion. A departmental screening committee meets twice a year to sanction proposals. Similar schemes are in force in many states to deal with stagnation.**

Not all ministries follow the traditional system of selection for higher posts. The scientific ministries have for a long time been operating a scheme of 'flexible complementing' to enable scientific and technical officers in designated organisations to move to higher grades on the basis of merit irrespective of the availability of vacancies in the higher grade. Performance is assessed by peer groups with regard to domain knowledge and demonstrated excellence in work on the basis of assessment records and interview.

The Ministry of Railways operates a merit-based selection scheme. Seventy per cent of posts in Group C are filled by selection from employees in the prescribed zone of consideration in the feeder grade. While promotion to the posts classified as selection posts is based on written test and interview, promotion to posts classified as non-selection posts is on the basis of seniority and suitability. The interview marks are based on professional ability, record of service, seniority, personality, leadership, educational qualification and performance in interview. Among state governments, Orissa is unique in following the system of supersession of seniority list by persons with higher than the benchmark in a panel.

There is frustration among central and state employees over the differential prospects of promotion for officers in different services and delays in the finalisation of panels. This leads to litigation over promotion and seniority list. For AIS and Group A officers, the Surendranath Committee has suggested improvements in the present system. The observations in the ACRs would be moderated to ensure consistency between the overall grading, the assessment against work performance, the assessment against different attributes and a pen picture of the officer. The criteria and process for promotion is: (a) satisfactory completion of all required training programmes; and (b) evaluation of the ACRs on a point scale.

Much concern is being expressed about the progressive displacement of the merit principle by the seniority criterion except in the top 2 per cent of posts. To counter this concern, it is useful to note that the original aim of the seniority principle in the colonial service was to insulate the promotion process both from the vagaries of politics and from the personal connections of individual employees. These risks may have largely disappeared in many developed countries, but they are still real in countries like India with a persisting danger of the politicisation of the civil service. Government considers it important, on balance, to give a progressively important role to merit considerations in promotion with careful attention to improvements in performance appraisal and employee perceptions of the fairness and consistency of the process.

### *Performance Incentives*

Since promotion is largely based on seniority, officials, especially those in the field such as collectors, look for non-monetary incentives either in the work environment or assignment of work, or for an opportunity to innovate and scale up innovation or the approbation of client groups. Central and state governments also recognise the need to minimise negative incentives relating to work environment, lack of infrastructure or the operation of extraneous influence in transfers and promotion.

Besides periodic increases in pay and allowances, state governments are experimenting with a variety of monetary and non-monetary incentives to promote greater motivation and to reward good performance at middle and senior levels. These include selection for isolated posts, preferred deputation to non-profit organisations, posts in international organisations and training in India and abroad. Andhra Pradesh is building in special incentives for superior performers in the online monitoring of performance of organisations and functionaries. The incentives include transfer and placement in preferred locations and positions, out-of-turn promotion, opportunity for higher education and awards. Middle and senior officers are equipped to become drivers of information technology through advanced training in institutes of management.

**Box 3.9 Recognising and Rewarding Merit**

Ministries like Railways and Posts follow a practice of recognising and rewarding merit and outstanding service in different service categories from Group D to Group A. Awards are given for outstanding achievement and exceptional service in each division and at the national level. Similar awards are given by other ministries such as the Ministries of Health, Education, Urban Development (for officers of central public works department) and Communications. Medals and awards are given to officers in the police service and central police organisations in special functions on Republic Day and other times. Presidential awards and citations are given to officers of different services every year. The Education Department honours teachers at national and state level. The rules provide for the grant of cash awards for distinguished achievement in the course of duty. Some incentives are common to all employees and include cash awards, advance increments, department-wide awards for best performance, and public recognition and out-of-turn promotion for Class III and IV employees in some cases.

## 3.10 Optimising Workforce Size and Deployment of Staff

### *The Fifth Central Pay Commission and After*

Starting with the report of the FCPC, the emphasis has been on a scientific approach to downsizing government staff. The FCPC Report outlined a fourfold comprehensive strategy to bring about control of workforce size, not necessarily in sequential steps:

- Reduction in the quantum of work by withdrawing from non-essential functions, transferring functions to state governments and corporate bodies, and contracting out tasks to the private sector, voluntary sector and autonomous agencies;
- Reduction in work to be performed due to organisational restructuring, such as reduction in ministries and departments, introduction of an officer-oriented system in public offices, delayering and level jumping and use of multi-skilled employees;
- Reduction of staff requirements due to computerisation, process re-engineering and system changes and moving towards a paperless office; and
- Direct rightsizing by the abolition of vacant posts, freeze on

recruitment, across-the-board cuts, statutory control on the creation of posts, attractive voluntary retirement scheme (VRS) and compulsory retirement.

Several measures such as hiring and recruitment freezes or abolition of vacant positions are already routinely practised in the central government and a number of Indian states. Since they affect potential and not actual employees, recruitment freezes are less politically contentious than other downsizing measures such as targeted or voluntary redundancies. The central Finance Ministry has abolished over 200,000 posts since the issue of economy instructions in 1992 while limiting the creation of new posts.

### *Implementing the Expenditure Reforms Commission Report*

Government appointed the Expenditure Reforms Commission (ERC) in 1999 to recommend steps for, *inter alia*, containing the cost of government employment and pensions in the central government. The ERC carried forward the suggestions of the FCPC in terms of institutionalised measures for downsizing the workforce and suggested the use of the budget instrument to ensure their enforcement. The ERC conducted functional reviews in 36 ministries and identified a potential surplus of over 100,000 posts. The reviews revealed that employees from Groups C and D accounted for 92 per cent of the total staff strength and that it was necessary to reduce this large support staff, while increasing the front-line staff. The ERC's recommendations on downsizing are contained in the section of the report on optimising government staff strength.

By its order in May 2001 and subsequent orders, government implemented the recommendation of the ERC for rationalising the organisational structure of ministries and for restricting future recruitment in government. These orders restricted new recruitment in central agencies to one-third the posts falling vacant by retirement, subject to a minimum of 1 percent of the total sanctioned strength of the Department. The orders are applicable also to statutory bodies and autonomous agencies fully or partially funded by government. Departments were directed to prepare Annual Direct Recruitment Plans covering the genuine requirements of all cadres, having regard to attrition rates, whether the cadres were managed by that ministry or department, or by the DOPT. Vacancies which remained unfilled for a year would be abolished. The task of preparing the Plan is undertaken in each ministry or department by a screening committee, headed by the Secretary of that ministry or department, with a representative from the DOPT and the Department of Expenditure. The annual recruitment plans for vacancies in Groups B, C and D can be cleared by the Departmental Committee. However, in the case of Group A services, the annual recruitment plan must be cleared by a committee headed by the Cabinet Secretary, with the secretary of the department concerned, the Secretary of the DOPT and the Secretary of the Department of Expenditure as members.

The downsizing policy is thus enforced by flexible department-specific exercises for annual recruitment plans based on an analysis of the prevailing organisational structure, changing workload, need to fill critical vacancies, identification of areas amenable to computerisation and scope for reorganisation where this is considered necessary. The recruiting authorities initiate recruitment only after the requisitioning authority assures them about the approval of the recruitment plan and non-availability of persons in the surplus staff cell. The exercise is reported to have yielded the surrender of about 80,000 vacant positions, including posts in key departments like the Ministries of Defence and Railways. If departments are able to save on manpower-related expenditure, the savings can be used on other expenditure of their choice, for example for purchase of equipment or foreign travel.

In the face of runaway growth in salary expenditure, the finance departments in the central and state governments have been enforcing a freeze on the creation of posts at all levels, besides abolishing vacant positions. Some states imposed across-the-board cuts in staff based on zero budget exercises similar to that undertaken in Maharashtra in the late 1980s. *De facto* or formal bans on direct recruitment have been enforced in Andhra Pradesh and a number of states since early 1990s. Some states have also banned the creation of work-charged posts. Usually, certain priority departments like elementary education, health and police are exempted from these instructions. To prevent the possibility of unauthorised creation, regularisation and continuance of posts, Andhra Pradesh enacted legislation to provide for imprisonment and fines for those violating the instructions.

Courts have consistently upheld the right of government to retrench staff following *bona fide* abolition of posts and to weed out incompetent or dishonest staff on the basis of tangible evidence. Where retrenchment takes place in an establishment owing to reduction of work or shrinkage of cadres, the principle of 'last in first out' is applied.

### *Public Enterprise Reform and VRS*

Central and state public enterprises employ approximately 9.7 million people out of a total Indian labour force of 406 million. The fiscal crisis in the 1990s stimulated new thinking on the reform and privatisation of public enterprises under central and state governments. The policy of the central government was to restructure and revive potentially viable public enterprises; close down public enterprises which cannot be revived and reduce government equity in all non-strategic public enterprises to 26 per cent or less, looking at each case on merit.

Public enterprises employ more people often because social obligations are imposed on them and they are subject to political direction. A difficult dimension of reform was the need to protect the interests of workers employed in the enterprises proposed for closure, sale or restructuring. The objectives of the manpower planning exercise to improve performance of public enterprises in central and state governments were:

- To achieve the optimum level of manpower in public enterprises with the desired average age mix so as to cope with the changing needs of society and the enterprises;
- To provide for necessary adjustment in manpower through redeployment so that all levels of skills and productivity are improved; and
- To compensate such manpower as may be rendered surplus in restructuring or in exercises taken up by the organisation, including winding up.

The officers and employees in Andhra Pradesh, for example, were offered three options: to be retained under new management; to be relieved from service after taking advantage of an attractive voluntary retirement scheme or to include one's name in the list of surplus candidates, kept with the surplus cell of state government.

The voluntary retirement scheme for public enterprise staff in central government and most states provided for an *ex gratia* amount for regular staff on varying terms, such as 35 to 45 days of emoluments for each year of qualifying service and 25 days for each year of balance service till retirement However, the ceiling was set in all cases by the emoluments for the months of service remaining before normal superannuation or subject to a minimum payment of around Rs. 250,00. The employee is also eligible to draw all terminal benefits. The orders uniformly directed the abolition of posts held by the retiring persons. The employee was barred from employment in any government department or public enterprise after opting for VRS.

### *Social Safety Net in Central and State Enterprises.*

The main components of the safety net to mitigate the social cost of retrenchment were counselling, retraining on a targeted basis and follow-up services to assist workers in finding alternative jobs or becoming self-employed. The Central Department of Public Enterprises launched a scheme for counselling, retraining and redeployment rationalised employees of central public sector enterprises. The scheme provides opportunities for the development of entrepreneurial skills so that the trained persons can start self-employment ventures or other income-generating activities. Counselling is intended to enable the employees to adjust to the new environment after the loss of their job. Fifteen nodal agencies were selected to conduct the survey of rationalised employees (including those who are about to be relieved) and identify persons willing to take advantage of the facilities provided by the scheme.

### *Special Voluntary Retirement Scheme for Employees in Central Government*

The existing rules contain provision for a voluntary retirement scheme for government servants after 20 years of eligible service with an attractive provision of an extra five years of service in calculating terminal benefits.

Government announced the special VRS after accepting the recommendation of the ERC. The DOPT and the Department of Pensions and Pensioner Welfare implement the scheme jointly and monitor the response to the scheme on the basis of proposals from departments regarding surplus staff and those opting for VRS. The newly constituted Division of Retraining and Redeployment in the DPPW is in charge of obtaining information from various departments about the staff identified as surplus, the extent of internal deployment, and the staff to be transferred to the surplus cell.

**Box 3.10 Special Scheme of Voluntary Retirement in Central Government**

**Following suggestions from the FCPC and the ERC, central government announced in February 2002 an attractive scheme for voluntary retirement similar to the scheme for the public enterprises, which was open for a limited period. The scheme is confined to permanent central government employees, who become surplus consequent to implementation of work studies, restructuring of departments, implementation of recommendations of the ERC, the abolition/ merger of departments and transfer of activity to lower levels of government or to the private sector.**

**This scheme was projected by government as part of its efforts to rightsize the civil service. The scheme provided for a liberal *ex gratia* payment of 35 days of basic pay and dearness allowance for each year of eligible service till the date of retirement and 25 days per year for the remaining period till normal superannuation, subject to a maximum of emoluments to be drawn till the age of normal retirement. The employee is further entitled to terminal benefits. This scheme supplemented the existing provisions for early retirement.**

### *VRS in States*

There is growing interest from many state governments in VRS schemes for the core civil service. A number are either considering or have recently implemented such schemes, including Karnataka, Madhya Pradesh, Orissa and Punjab. The state of Goa implemented a VRS scheme over 2000–2002, which led to a reduction in the government workforce of around 2,565, or 5.3 per cent. The cost of the programme to date has been Rs. 1.5 billion, or approximately $13,021 per retrenched worker. Orissa government kept the scheme open to all employees subject to the right of government to refuse applications in the public interest. Orissa provided a separate voluntary separation scheme for work-charged and daily wage staff with a different rate of compensation.

### *Redeployment and Surplus Staff Cells*

Central government and some states consider the identification and deployment of surplus staff to be part of an integrated exercise for rationalising manpower within and across departments and the agencies under them. The exercise involves identifying surplus staff, monitoring the movement of staff with the help of a robust HRM database, setting up a dedicated and well-equipped cell for managing the surplus staff and matching it against vacant posts, arranging for training, and ensuring a credible and efficient process of redeployment. The surplus staff cell is also expected to ensure the existence of contingent plans in departments to fill up vacancies caused by the exit of employees in critically deficient areas.

A scheme for redeployment of surplus staff has been in operation in the central government since 1966. About 14,000 surplus employees from different categories had been redeployed by 2001. Following the VRS order in 2002, government announced a sequence of steps to be followed by departments to identify and declare surplus staff in different categories. The departments should transfer surplus staff to the Retraining and Redeployment Division (RRD) in the Ministry of Personnel after exhausting efforts for internal deployment. RRD was reconstituted out of the erstwhile surplus staff cell and the unit in Labour Ministry. The division will handle surplus staff from all categories instead of the earlier arrangement for a different agency for Group D.

Central rules for deployment of surplus staff enable the employee to be posted in any cadre in any department of the central government. The rules also enable the employee to be appointed to a post carrying a lower scale if no equivalent post is available, with the promise of adjustment to a higher post at a later stage. The recruiting agencies are required to consider candidates offered by the surplus cell before considering persons from the open market. A committee has been set up in the Ministry of PPGP to work out the training activities to be undertaken to retrain the employees to occupy posts for which they might not be currently fitted.

Andhra Pradesh set up a surplus staff cell in the Finance Department following the enactment of legislation to prevent unauthorised appointment and regularisation in 1994. The staff is mostly from Groups C and D as well as from work-charged categories. The staff could be deployed on a permanent or temporary basis within or outside the district, including village panchayats, subject to legal constraints on transferring staff outside districts. Powers of redeployment and training have been delegated to district collectors. Both Andhra Pradesh and Maharashtra provide for the compulsory discharge of the employee if he or she does not accept alternative employment or does not opt for VRS. The employee in the surplus cell in Maharashtra can be posted anywhere in the state and in any cadre with an equivalent payscale, subject to liberal approaches for staff in district cadres. The effort to monitor the identification and placement of surplus staff is to be bolstered by the establishment of a centralised database for employees, as described above.

### *Problems and Options*

Voluntary retirement schemes for redundant employees typically suffer from problems of cost, adverse selection and re-entry of the retired employees. As regards separation costs, these could prove to be expensive for cash-strapped central and state governments. Even allowing for government's right to accept or reject a request for voluntary retirement, the risk of adverse selection would be greater in government as it is difficult to devise screening mechanisms to retain the more qualified, honest and sincere people. Further, in conformity with court rulings, government has to place staff in the surplus cell, starting with the most junior person. In the orders issued by states, those opting for voluntary retirement are banned from re-employment in any department or PSU. A similar provision may be needed in central government.

The central voluntary retirement scheme is considered to lack sting in the absence of any provision (as proposed by ERC) for the retrenchment of persons who fail to opt for the scheme within a prescribed period. There have been few applications for VRS in the light of the attraction of staying on in public service till superannuation. There are limited opportunities for alternative employment in the private sector for government employees with mainly secretariat skills.

Consistent with international experience, central and state governments have realised that schemes for voluntary retirement should be the last step in a set of sequenced options for rightsizing and that too much reliance on response to VRS will be ineffective, however attractively packaged the scheme is. A critical element of this strategy is the systematic functional review of departments to identify surplus staff.

At the same time, governments are continuing the thrust to enforce a recruitment freeze and measures for targeted and compulsory redundancy in order to bring about the desired reduction in manpower. Government would continue to enforce checks on future recruitment and the creation of unnecessary new posts by ministries and autonomous agencies.

The near-term options for rightsizing are less painful, costly and controversial but will still help organisations reduce their wage bill. These are part of the HRM strategy for ensuring meritocracy and for clearing the deadwood from public service. They include the following:

- Regular and rigorous implementation of executive instructions for the premature retirement of government employees at the age of 50 or 55 on the basis of screening of performance under existing rules;
- Installing a more open, effective and credible system of performance assessment and benchmarking in ACRs, or implementing practices such as an efficiency bar, on the basis of which poor-performing employees can be regularly retired from service;
- Phasing out compassionate appointments;
- Developing a time-bound action plan for disengaging large numbers of work-charged and daily wage employees, and addressing problems in existing appointment practices for temporary or casual labour that lead to the court-mandated absorption of employees;
- Improving mechanisms for establishment control to prevent unauthorised recruitment into the civil service; and
- Streamlining and accelerating departmental enquiries against government employees facing major punishments, and revising employee grievance procedures.

## 3.11 Enhancing Staff Training and Development

### *National Training Policy*

Central and state governments see a key role for training in improving employee performance in congruence with organisational goals, assisting in preparation of the employees for higher or altered responsibilities, and in increasing employees' accountability to citizens. This is reflected in the objectives of the National Training Policy of 1996 and a number of state training policies, besides sector strategies for improved implementation of programmes. Training is increasingly seen in central ministries and progressive states as an integral part of personnel management, and linked to recruitment, career and promotional avenues, human resource development, and general environment of governmental functioning.

**Box 3.11 National Training Policy of India**

**The objectives of the National Training Policy (April 1996) are to:**

- **Enhance professional knowledge and skills to achieve the better performance of organisations and individuals;**
- **Sensitise personnel to the professional, socio-economic and political environment and inculcate the right attitudes;**
- **Make the training programmes focus on responsiveness, commitment, awareness of economic and social developments and technological changes, infusion of scientific temper and accountability.**

Training would cover both entry-level and in-service training at suitable intervals in an employee's career, besides training for competence-building and orientation before moving into posts of higher and/or varied responsibility. Given the large numbers of persons to be trained, working in diverse environments and organisational cultures, emphasis has been placed on decentralised and demand-based training, so as to cover all employees over a definite period.

To supervise the implementation of the policy, the DOPT set up a National Training Council under the Minister, with representatives from central and state departments and experts. The strategy will be operationalised through installing committed training managers in each department or office, effective training of trainers, augmenting training infrastructure at the national, state and regional levels, and building networks of training institutions of different sectors, experts and resource persons from the civil service and outside.

Given the low priority given to training and low budget allocation in many states, the impetus of central allocations has been a key factor in ensuring minimum level of training for supervisory cadres and front-line staff, and also for upgrading the standards of state training institutions. Central government also assists states by channelling foreign technical assistance grants and facilitating collaboration of state agencies with overseas academic institutions. Besides training programmes for the All India Services and central services within and outside India, central ministries have been assisting the training of state general services and specialised cadres in different sectors over the years, and the magnitude of this effort has increased in the last decade. The central Department of Personnel and Training is the nodal agency for implementing the training policy. Individual central ministries are encouraged to formulate and implement training programmes for the functional cadres under them, and to operate their own training institutions. Efforts have been made to ensure that 1.5 per cent of the salary budget of each department is earmarked for implementing the training plan. Many central and state initiatives in training have been taken during the last five years in the context of the national policy, and these actions have benefited the state governments as well. These include:

- Advocating the adoption of state training policies through meetings of state officials and directors in charge of training, dissemination of good examples, support to exercises for training needs assessment, and building up a cadre of resource persons in training;
- Bringing together and networking different central functional training institutes, on the one hand, and different state administrative training institutes (ATIs) and national level institutes, on the other, for sharing experience and trainer resources, training methodology, integrated training of personnel from different departments and feedback to policy-makers;
- Grants for general and specific category programmes, which are conducted though a range of public and private training institutions, for senior and middle level officials of central and state governments and public sector undertakings, on general skills and specific themes of development administration, organisation development, information technology, gender issues, human rights, citizen orientation, tackling corruption and training of trainers;
- An ambitious training programme undertaken by the Ministry of Rural Development for state and district level training of all the elected representatives and functionaries in panchayat raj institutions to supplement the individual efforts of states;
- Support from central ministries, as a part of centrally sponsored schemes and externally aided projects, to institutes of state agencies and NGOs for training specific categories of state staff, such as

teachers, health workers, pre-school workers, family welfare staff, functionaries of Panchayat Raj Institutions (PRIs) and municipalities, personnel of functional agencies, and personnel in infrastructure and development;

- Training in emerging issues of globalisation, world trade and deregulation, electronic governance, disaster management and ethical values, often with the help of business and civil society;
- Specific programmes for building the capacities of voluntary agencies and community-based organisations and self-help groups under different sector programmes and poverty alleviation projects;
- In-service training programmes for IAS officers in Lal Bahadur Shastri National Academy of Administration (LBSNAA), Administrative Training Institutes, Indian Institutes of Management (IIMs), and other reputable private institutes, at different stages of officers' careers;
- Similar programmes for officials of many central services, management development programmes for senior state officials, and training programmes, sometimes with the collaboration of overseas training institutions;
- Training for public sector executives at the Administrative Staff College of India (ASCI), Institute of Public Enterprise, Management Development Institute and IIMs;
- Focus on the training of trainers and upgrading state and district level institutes, including innovative methods of decentralised training and distance learning;
- Taking the initiative in setting up regional training centres in a number of sectors such as urban development, rural development, public health engineering and environment;
- Developing a movement for total quality management in training institutions and taking steps to build their capacities in different ways with the help of Plan grants and access to international assistance;
- Finalisation of steps to conduct a graduate diploma programme in public policy (from 2002) for senior officials of different services in the Indian Institute of Management, Bangalore, on the model of the course at the Kennedy School of Government, Harvard;

- Development of training programmes in a number of state training centres and LBSNAA for sensitising central and state officials to gender issues and the establishment of a Centre for Gender Studies;
- Support for the formulation of training modules to fortify the thrust for citizen-centred, honest and transparent governance and TQM on the lines of the action plan approved by a conference of Chief Ministers in May 1997.

### *Training Activities of Central Government*

The training Division of the DOPT provides support to state governments and central agencies in organising training programmes, training infrastructure, faculty development and sharing of resources. The two major training institutions under the DOPT are LBSNAA and the Institute of Secretariat Training and Management. LBSNAA is the premier national training and research institution for the career training of IAS officers including senior officers at the level of joint secretary and above. Excellent post-entry and in-service training is provided by the training institutions under different ministries, such as the Railway Staff College, National Police Academy, Institute for Audit and Accounts, Postal Services Training Institute, Income Tax Services Institute, National Institute of Rural Development and Central Institute of Road Transport.

The ISTM designs and conducts post-entry foundation, refresher and specialised training programmes for different grades of secretariat officers up to the middle management level and personal assistants at the induction and post-entry level. It is also the lead institute in training for trainers and has emerged as a 'Centre of Excellence' in many other specialised areas of training. A number of state organisations have approached the ISTM to provide them with training support. The ISTM provides faculty support for state governments and union territory administrations through peripatetic training programmes and assistance in designing their training courses through training of trainers and DTS programmes, courses in behavioural skills, financial management and office management.

The Indian Institute of Public Administration (IIPA), New Delhi, is an autonomous agency, which was established by government following the report of Paul Appleby on Indian administration. It promotes the study of public administration, economic and political sciences and undertakes training and research in public administration. The DOPT and other ministries provide support to the Institute for training programmes and in specific areas like disaster management.

The DOPT supports training courses in eminent national centres of administration like the IIPA, Administrative Staff College and IIMs to develop policy skills and leadership qualities in middle and top officers from various senior executive services. LBSNAA co-ordinates and supports the TQM initiative in training. The courses on the training of trainers are an essential step in developing the competence of trainers through programmes in Direct Trainer Skills (DTS), Design of Training (DoT), Master Trainers Course and Management of Training (MoT). These special modules aim to improve trainers' abilities, delivery skills, designing skills for subject specific courses, internal and external validation and to provide exposure to the effective use of audio visual aids. Trainers developed under the Trainer Development Project are called Recognised Users (RUs), who are recognised by the government to deliver Direct Trainer Skills and Design of Training courses. The National Informatics Centre and other eminent institutions organise programmes on the use of computer tools in administration.

**_Box 3.12_ UNDP Assisted Project for Strengthening Training Capacity**

**With the help of UNDP, the training division is implementing a programme for strengthening the capacity of 17 selected state administrative training institutes. Support is extended for the analysis of training needs, development of an employee database, faculty development, development of training modules and curricula, computer infrastructure and online sharing of resources. Over 45 subject specific training modules have been developed together with the training of resource persons to ensure the quality of training. A tool kit for the assessment of training needs and the evaluation of training programmes has been developed. Major emphasis has been placed on the use of the distance learning method so that training can be taken closer to the workplace of employees at the cutting edge, rather than strain the limited resources of training institutions. In the context of the legislation for freedom of information, a sub-programme aims at operationalising the law, ensuring exposure to grassroots initiatives and building the capacity and sensitivity of the public authorities for improving citizens' access to information.**

Following the implementation of another project targeted at women in the civil service, a core group of resource persons for training and research in different departments was developed who have been trained in reputable institutions in India and abroad. Special training programmes for cadre-control authorities and employees in central and state agencies have been organised following ten regional workshops and the preparation of region-specific curricula. A module for distance learning in this area has been prepared for all state employees.

### *Training for IAS and Senior Officers*

A unique feature of the training of IAS officers after entry into the service is the foundation course and the sandwich programme comprising two phases. The integrated foundation courses for the AIS and Group A services impart a basic understanding of the constitutional, political, socio-economic and legal framework, develop basic values in officers and provide collective spirit among all services.

The first phase of the sandwich professional programme in LBSNAA consists of 24 weeks; it aims to develop professional competence in handling the wide range of responsibilities in the early years of service. Besides knowledge of public administration and management, law, economics and computer literacy, the course is also aimed at strengthening the understanding of the political and social environment in which the IAS officer has to function and at developing service values. Officers benefit from attachments to the army, public sector organisations and voluntary agencies. The officers are then sent to districts in the allotted state for extensive on-the-job training to get a feel for administration. The officers then come back to the Academy for the second phase of six weeks when training is issue- and problem-oriented and an opportunity is given to examine field realities in relation to theoretical inputs. The officer is required to pass an examination at the end of the first and second phases to be confirmed in service.

Under the present system of in-service training for IAS officers, every IAS officer is required to attend training programmes in common themes of one-week duration or policy-based programmes of longer duration in LBSNAA or various eminent Indian institutions. They can attend one more training programme in a financial year, at their choice, in 22 public and private training institutions and national institutes of management. The courses for those with 6–9 years service cover programme implementation, courses for those with 10–16 years service cover decision making, and courses for those with 17–20 years service cover policy planning and analysis. The themes include infrastructure development, institutional finance, computer application, operational research, WTO and trade issues, ethical values, public-private partnership, urban development, disaster management, leadership and change management, state finances and deregulation. There is increasing integration of the training of AIS and central services. Besides the foundation course for all new recruits in LBSNAA, joint courses are often conducted for in-service officers belonging to services like the IAS, IPS, IFOS and central services.

Government is acting on the recommendations of the Surendranath Committee to enhance the skills and capability of officers of AIS and central services. It is envisaged that all services must specify career-training programmes, which would be mandatory for promotion to different levels. These training programmes would aim to equip an officer with the necessary skills for the positions likely to be held in the next 9–10 years. Accordingly, compulsory training programmes at suitably timed stages of the officer's career would be conducted. Performance in these programmes would be taken into account for the next promotion besides efforts made by the officer to improve their qualifications and skills.

Consistent with this strategy, training of IAS officers will be increasingly modulated to suit career shifts in the district and state administrations and central government. There will be four levels of career building at the stage of 7, 14, 21 and 28 years service, corresponding respectively to skill building and project management, policy formulation, policy analysis and strategic planning leadership, team building and management. Each course is planned to be of 13 weeks duration and government would call upon LBSNAA, the IIMs, the ASCI and eminent private institutions to anchor the module for different phases related to the job requirements for each phase and the capability of the training institute.

Government is identifying 11 domains for streaming the assignment of officers for selection to posts under the Central Staffing Scheme, other than posts meant for particular services, such as central police organisations and the IFOS. Different central departments have been placed in one or more domains.

Following reduced funding for foreign training from donor agencies, government has introduced the scheme of domestic funding of foreign training This covers both long- and short-term training in reputable universities and institutes in several countries. A scheme of partial funding of foreign studies has also been started, where officers are provided with financial assistance for pursuing studies and instruction in Indian and foreign universities. Deputation for foreign courses would be linked to the domain of the candidate and the officer's potential for future assignment.

**Box 3.13 Alternative Training Providers**

**Government agencies are increasingly reaching out to private and voluntary agencies and expanding the universe of training providers. The Institutes of Management and the Administrative Staff College conduct executive development programmes for public sector and government employees while many scientific institutes like the Indian Institute of Science help in environmental training. Business associations such as the Confederation of Indian Industries and FICCI have assisted government in designing and conducting training programmes for total quality management, transferring best practices in private sector training programmes, as well as courses in new topics like WTO protocols, intellectual property, copyright laws and cyber laws. A research group in Bangalore called the Public Affairs Agency is training public officials in re-engineering procedures and responsive interaction with citizens, while another group in Bangalore is helping municipalities to install fund based accounting systems. There are similar examples in other cities and rural areas.**

### State Initiatives

Andhra Pradesh and Maharashtra are among the few states which have consciously sought to locate the policies for training and HRD in an overall strategy for civil service reform and administrative improvement. Maharashtra's training institute YASHADA also hosts training centres for rural and urban development, a centre for good governance and a centre for ethical values. Government has encouraged the institute to develop its capacity for policy advice, functional reviews and citizen-centred administration.

**_Box 3.14_ Human Resource Development in Andhra Pradesh**

**The Andhra Pradesh Government has designated its HRD Institute as the nodal centre for all training in the state. The governing board is headed by the Chief Minister. The Institute's activities are supported by a high quality staff and an adequate budget. The three significant points that make the Institute stand out among Indian states is: 1) the integration of training with performance improvement at all levels; 2) the equal stress on content and training delivery; and 3) expanding the boundaries of training to promote governing for results at middle and senior levels. There is a strategic shift in the role of the HRD Institute from direct provision of training to training of trainers, upgrading capacities of sector institutes, electronic governance, overseeing decentralised training, impact evaluation and linking HRD to Vision 2020 goals and cross-sector issues.**

**The training strategy is based on full involvement of all departments and agencies in various ways, such as support for sector institutes, the change agents programme, training needs analysis and the preparation of manuals on departmental functions and tasks of various functionaries with consultant support from the Institute. The HRD Institute also supervises the training of around 300 middle and senior level officers as chief information officers to steer electronic governance in different departments. The Institute is networking with other leading Indian institutes for public policy and training and with international institutes.**

Government personnel in Andhra Pradesh have been divided for training into four groups, namely policy-level functionaries such as ministers and secretaries (about 100 people), administrative level functionaries (about 800 AIS officers and heads of departments), executive level functionaries or change agents (such as revenue and development functionaries who number around 10,000 people), and a support group of about 450,000 employees. The duration, type of training and delivery mode are structured according to the target group. The trainers are placed in all the district centres under the management of district officers.. The general training is complemented by skill-based training provided in departmental institutes for irrigation, public works, health, education, etc.

In a number of states, for example Karnataka and Tamil Nadu, there are institutes for training secretariat staff and a network of district level training centres for revenue and block employees, which are supervised by the Revenue Department. These centres have been placed under the technical supervision of the ATI. Besides these centres for general support staff, training centres have been set up, often with support from central ministries and donor agencies, in different states for primary and secondary teachers, health staff and various technical departments. Staff training is often organised by individual functional agencies such as electricity boards, transport corporations, industrial development agencies, housing and development authorities and water supply agencies.

The computerisation of the traditional operations of government has revealed the scope for drawing on the ferment of new learning among younger employees. The CARD (computerised aid to registration of documents) programme of Andhra Pradesh relied for its success on the on-the-job instruction of workers in computerisation and scanning of documents and their acceptance of the transition to non-manual systems to reduce the drudgery of paper-based systems. Karnataka's *Bhoomi* (computerised land records) programme relied on the training of traditional village accountants and revenue inspectors in the new system.

Under the stimulus of central funding and state leadership, a major programme of training for all elected representatives in panchayati raj institutions in rural areas is in progress in all the states. This training is co-ordinated by the National Institute of Rural Development and state institutes. In providing decentralised training for over 500,000 elected representatives and officials in local government in Andhra Pradesh, the DVD-based training for the district centres is supplemented by KU band training kit through the recently established APNET. Karnataka has inducted voluntary agencies in the design and conduct of training programmes in innovative ways to achieve the learning and awareness of women representatives and less literate persons. The learning experience is sustained by peer learning and associations of local leaders of panchayats and women's groups. Voluntary agencies play a significant role in the training of teachers and health workers as well as urban community workers in many states.

The thrust for citizen-oriented administration has led to new initiatives for training focused on increasing the responsiveness and accountability of officials, especially those at the cutting edge. Training modules have been devised for citizen's charters and public grievance redress with common topics and themes appropriate to the specific functions of departments. After the enactment of the law on freedom of information, central and state governments are poised to train and reorient officers on record management, retrieval and disclosure of documents and dealing quickly with demands for information in urban and rural areas.

### *Challenges*

Despite the scale and diversity of training programmes at central and state level, the capacity of training programmes has fallen short of the huge numbers of personnel to be trained or needing reorientation, partly due to shortage of resources and infrastructure. Networking among central institutes for different services is admittedly still weak, as is the collaboration of sector institutes in the states with each other and with the ATIs. Training institutions are not able to attract qualified candidates for their faculties from public services or academic institutions due to low pay, though the deficiency is made up by inducting officers with an interest in training. There are inadequate mechanisms for assessing the effectiveness of training programmes. State governments, with a few exceptions, do not accord adequate priority to training and budgetary provision is limited. Government is also concerned that training has tended to concentrate disproportionately on senior personnel and that training tends to be supply-driven.

The central training division is addressing these and similar concerns of building competence and networking of training institutions, while replicating best practices elsewhere for evaluating the impact of training activities. It is establishing a web-based learning and resource network for networking central and state institutes besides national institutes of excellence. The experience of Andhra Pradesh points the way for expanding the spread and quality of training. The DOPT and a number of central and state training institutions have initiated TQM practices in 11 selected training institutions, with LBSNAA as the lead institute. As for the financial crunch, national financial institutions like HUDCO and NABARD provide technical assistance for upgrading the capability of project personnel, while a number of centrally funded programmes for rural development and infrastructure contain financial provisions for training field staff and people's committees.

## 3.12 Enhancing Skills for Policy-making and Co-ordination

### *Enhancing Policy Skills*

As expert committees have pointed out, government needs arms-length centres, where ideas can be bounced around by people with knowledge and practical experience, and ways to link these deliberative councils to decision-making structures. However, getting policy advice calls for changes in systems of making policy and cross-sector working within government. The Indian Government has increasingly played a role in enabling these think tanks to develop and in building internal capacity within government departments. Government hopes to use the emerging centres of public policy to distil policy issues and options and disseminate policy briefs in intelligible terms in order to increase public awareness and debate on vital issues. Central government constituted a working group in 1997 to make proposals for setting up a long-term programme in public policy in a selected institution. The Group's recommendation led to the government's decision to set up a Centre for Public Policy in Bangalore in 2000 with UNDP support to conduct a graduate diploma programme for public policy for senior officials, to organise executive development programmes and to undertake relevant research. A central grant assists the Centre's activities in research and outreach, documentation and diffusion of innovation. Following a first programme for about 50 officers in the best traditions of international programmes, the Centre is now organising a second programme.

The Planning Commission decided to set up a centre for public policy and governance in the Institute for Applied Manpower Research (IAMR). The centre will undertake applied studies, and organise international workshops and exchanges. It is developing into a clearing-house for public policy with links to different policy institutes and training institutions. The National Institute of Administrative Research society was set up under LBSNAA to undertake and co-ordinate research and development activities related to public policy. Its activities include research studies, consultancy services, development of training modules and the preparation of case studies.

**_Box 3.15_ Domain Competency**

**Streaming officers into particular domains is a key step in accomplishing the objective of orienting training according to the changing job profile of IAS officers. In government's perception, domain competency relates to sufficient background in a certain context of policy-making. It differs from general skills of policy/ programme formulation in that such general skills would relate primarily to knowledge of formal techniques of policy analysis/ programme formulation and experience of policy/ programme formulation generally. On the other hand, 'Domain Competence' will involve, in addition, significant subject matter knowledge, gained from work experience, academic study, training and research.**

## 3.13 Integrity and A Public Service Code of Conduct

### *Strategy for Tackling Corruption*

Governments at the central and state level have been concerned about the pernicious influence of corruption at various levels of government. The effect of corruption on the economy and public administration is obvious. An important feature of personnel management is the maintenance of professional ethics and upgrading the standards of administration. Elimination of corruption is seen as an element of good governance since accountability is the basic condition for not only preventing the misuse of official position but also for ensuring the application of public resources with the greatest degree of effectiveness and prudence.

The DOPT is the nodal agency for formulating government policy for the maintenance of integrity in the public services and the eradication of corruption, but all ministries and public agencies have a direct responsibility for ensuring discipline and integrity by preventive measures and working towards the elimination of corruption. The principal agencies for this purpose are the Central Vigilance Commission and the Central Bureau of Investigation. The DOPT is responsible for the appointment of chief vigilance officers in government agencies.

A calendar of vigilance action has been drawn up by the DOPT which specifies the targets to be accomplished by administrative authorities and public undertakings in vigilance. The annual plan of the department focuses on analysing and improving the continuous interplay of three elements – institutions, the delivery mechanism and the supportive framework of rules and procedures. There is a sub-plan for reviewing existing regulations and procedures so that functionaries and the public are not hindered by complicated procedures. The existing mechanism for monitoring vigilance cases and disciplinary proceedings has been revamped with computerised software.

Recent years have witnessed a number of positive measures in central and state governments such as the passage of the law relating to the Central Vigilance Commissioner, the introduction of legislation for setting up a central Ombudsman (Lok Pal), the strengthening of the institutions of ombudsman (Lok Ayuktha) and vigilance commissioner in the states, tightening of the provisions relating to prevention of corruption and the vigorous and independent functioning of anti-corruption agencies such as the Central Bureau of Investigation (CBI). The Lok Pal legislation enables government to proceed vigorously in cases of allegations against ministers and public functionaries through an independent institution with adequate resources.

In the strategy for curbing corruption, government is focusing equal attention on prevention, surveillance and deterrence and on dealing ruthlessly with the nexus of criminal elements and public functionaries. A recent amendment to electoral law obliges all candidates in central, state and local elections to declare their criminal antecedents, prosecution for offences and prior punishment. Government is eliminating any scope in the rules for any interference in the prompt prosecution and punishment of corrupt public servants. Though prior approval of government is required in the case of officers of the level of joint secretaries and above and the top officers of public undertakings, permission for prosecution in *prima facie* cases will be given within a stipulated period.

Central government and a number of states have strengthened their vigilance and anti-corruption machinery through the grant of independence and autonomy and provision of an adequate budget, staff and computerisation of operations. The details of their operations have been placed on the internet and submitted to the legislature through annual reports. Special courts have been set up to follow fast track procedures for ensuring speedy decisions.

All cases of proven holding of assets disproportionate to known sources of income of public servants are investigated and prosecuted. All civil servants are obliged to submit annual returns of immovable property to enable scrutiny by vigilance officers. It has been proposed that property acquired by public servants by illegal or corrupt means not only in their own names but also in the names of family members, could be attached and forfeited through amended legal provisions. Some states have announced the intention to enact such a law.

Various preventive steps have been contemplated and implemented to bring down the scope and incidence of corruption, especially at the cutting edge of administration. The stress is on factors such as secrecy, cumbersome procedures and unnecessary controls. Areas of discretion available to various levels of administration have been progressively reduced, along with guidelines to prevent their arbitrary use in fields such as tax assessment, valuation, allotment of outlets by public monopolies, housing, issue of licences and building permission. Simplification and liberalisation of excessive restrictions would reduce red tape, while deregulation and alternative delivery of services would minimise the delays and scope for corruption in areas of public monopoly. Independent regulating agencies would oversee the activities of private providers to protect public interest.

The role and powers of audit have been strengthened through the independent operation of the C&AG and the efforts of legislative committees for public accounts to pursue large and small irregularities and scams. Internal controls and audit have been strengthened in many states as in central government through public statements of financial accountability. Arrangements are in place to strengthen the networking of various agencies concerned with the prevention of waste and irregularity such as the C&AG, revenue collection agencies, CBI, Vigilance Commissioner and Lok Ayuktha.

Transparency and accountability in areas of interface with the public are being promoted though the laws on freedom of information and the Citizen's Charter as well as encouragement of citizen oversight. Agencies have been instructed to computerise procurement operations and display full transparency and predictability in procurement and contracts. A number of states have passed laws for transparency in procurement. E-governance is expected to reduce the incidence of corruption at the cutting edge.

The scope for collusion of corrupt officials with political leaders will be reduced and the civil services will be insulated from extraneous influence through transparency and objectivity in transfer policies as described earlier. All departments have been instructed to review the integrity and performance of officials periodically on the basis of evidence from different sources so that delinquent officers can be retired compulsorily without the need for lengthy enquiry. Officials at all levels have been encouraged to bring irregularities or suspected corruption to the notice of the Cabinet Secretary or Chief Secretary. The existing procedures for departmental enquiries and vigilance proceedings are being revamped as described in the next section.

### *Code of Ethics*

The thrust of civil service regulations is to restore public faith in the civil service by ensuring the commitment of government servants to ethical standards and the basic principles of the Constitution. Similar codes of ethics are envisaged for everyone in public life. The Prevention of Corruption Act and the Indian Penal Code contain the basic legal provisions for proceeding against corruption in public service and are supplemented by various regulations. The Central Civil Services (Conduct) Rules and similar rules notified by ministries like the Ministry of Railways specify the expectations of government servants and areas of misconduct. The state governments have notified similar rules for their employees.

The Ministry of Personnel, Public Grievances and Pensions has formulated a draft code of ethics endorsed by the Chief Ministers' Conference and this is currently being given a legal shape. The objective of the code is to prescribe standards of integrity and conduct which should prevail in the public services. It would apply to all services, general and technical. The proposed code will be in addition to the existing conduct rules. The State Governments of Gujarat, Madhya Pradesh and West Bengal have also drafted a Code of Ethics for civil servants.

### *Central Vigilance Agencies*

The Central Vigilance Commission was set up as an advisory body by executive instruction in 1964, in the aftermath of the Santhanam Committee's report on public sector corruption. Following directions from the Supreme Court, the CVC's role and mandate was expanded

### *Box 3.16* Code of Ethics for the Civil Service

**Every government servant is expected to maintain absolute integrity, political neutrality and devotion to duty at all times and to do nothing which is unbecoming in a government servant. He is expected to display promptness and courtesy to the public and avoid dilatory tactics. He should not use his position or influence to secure employment or other benefit for any member of his family. Government servants are barred from membership of any political party or from assisting any political activity. They are expected to avoid any criticism of government through printed or electronic media. They should not accept any gift or permit any family member to accept any gift except in stipulated circumstances and exceeding a small value. They should avoid unauthorised communication of information in confidential documents and abide by provisions of the Official Secrets Act (this is being relaxed following the law on freedom of information).**

**Government servants are expected to avoid becoming insolvent. They should not engage in any private trade or employment and should seek government permission for any commercial employment for a period of two years after retirement.**

**Misconduct leading to punishment would include wilful insubordination or disobedience, infidelity, sexual harassment, dishonesty, moral turpitude, disorderly behaviour, habitual lack of punctuality, neglect of work, incitement to strike and criminal conviction.**

to subsume supervision of anti-corruption work. Parliament passed a law in 2003 to give statutory shape and independence to the CVC. The CVC is now a three-member commission, headed by a Central Vigilance Commissioner with the status of the chairman of the UPSC. The CVC is conceived to be the apex vigilance institution, free of control from any executive authority, monitoring all vigilance activity under the central government and advising various authorities in central government organisations on planning, executing, reviewing and reforming their vigilance work. The CVC has been entrusted with the supervision of the Central Bureau of Investigation, including the investigation and prosecution of public servants for offences under the Prevention of Corruption Act. The CVC conducts a technical audit of construction works of governmental organisations from a vigilance angle. There are 15 posts of Commissioners for Departmental Enquiries (CDI) in the Commission.

In the ethics area, the CVC works with all government agencies on their programmes of 'vigilance' against corruption, providing guidance and monitoring implementation. Like the US Office of Government Ethics, the CVC has units for vigilance under the charge of part- or full-time chief vigilance officers within each ministry and within nationalised banks and public sector undertakings. The Commission is empowered to enquire or cause enquiries to be conducted into offences alleged to have been committed under the Prevention of Corruption Act, 1988 by Group A officers and senior officials of public sector undertakings and local authorities under the control of central government. In addition, the CVC scrutinises transactions by public officials that may be improper, receives and addresses complaints of corruption and abuse of power, refers enquiries to the CBI, and monitors the CBI's investigation and prosecution of offences under the Prevention of Corruption Act.

The Chief Vigilance Officers constitute an important link between the organisations concerned and the Central Vigilance Commission (as does the CBI). CVOs are expected to undertake both preventive and investigative functions. Government has issued executive instructions for the consultation of the CVC in all enquiries at the stage of deciding on departmental enquiry or prosecution and at the final stage of deciding on the quantum of punishment. The Establishment Officer obtains vigilance clearance from the CVC before submitting proposals to the ACC for the appointment of candidates on the panel for posts in ministries and public sector undertakings.

The CVC has issued instructions relating to transparency and probity in procurement. It has issued a circular stating that all authorities under its jurisdiction should publish on noticeboards and by other means the details of all cases regarding tenders and out-of-turn allotments or discretion exercised in favour of an employee or party. As for external scrutiny of the CVC, its Annual Report to the President and Parliament offers one avenue for oversight, and it issues frequent press releases besides information on its website.

### *Vigilance in States*

In every Indian state, there is either a State Vigilance Commission or Lok Ayuktha (ombudsman) which looks after the vigilance matters of the state governments. However, the state vigilance machinery does not enjoy the statutory status and independence of the CVC. Most vigilance commissioners report to the executive and are obliged to seek prior permission for investigating senior officers. Some state vigilance commissioners oversee the work of the anti-corruption wing of the police as in Andhra Pradesh. There is a similar network of chief vigilance officers reporting to the Vigilance Commissioner in the states. Experience shows that as the CVC gains political and public credibility, as well as increased authority and independence, some of the state-level bodies have also gained greater visibility and powers.

Lok Ayuktha, the state-level ombudsman, was thus established as an early response to accusations of corruption and maladministration against people in high places. Many states such as Orissa, Andhra Pradesh, Karnataka, Madhya Pradesh, Maharashtra, Tamil Nadu, Uttar Pradesh, Bihar, Rajasthan and Kerala have enacted legislation to establish the institution of a Lok Ayuktha (ombudsman), the latest being the new state of Chhattisgarh. The Lok Ayuktha enquires into various complaints directly received or referred to it by government and recommends prosecution or departmental enquiry against the concerned official or in some cases punitive action against ministers.

**_Box 3.17_ Success of Karnataka Lok Ayuktha**

**The Karnataka experience shows that an active and well-endowed ombudsman can effectively deter corruption and offer credible channels of grievance redress. The Vigilance Department functions under the Lok Ayuktha. The present incumbent is a retired Justice of the Supreme Court and he is appointed for a fixed term of five years in consultation with the Leader of the Opposition and the Chief Justice of the High Court. The enabling law vests the office with wide statutory powers ranging from investigating corruption and initiating prosecution to addressing grievances at any level of government, including the Chief Minister. Lok Ayuktha has a large complement of over 500 officers covering the police, technical, audit and statistical wings and a large budget. New positions of Vigilance Director have been created for the police, health and education, and large agencies like the Bangalore Development Authority. The Lok Ayuktha and his team have been very active in investigating waste and corruption in services affecting the public. The vigilance operations have been aided by computerised lodging and tracking of complaints. The growing activism of the Lok Ayuktha has obliged many departments to provide effective redress of public grievances and improve services to avoid adverse media attention and enquiry. The focus on enforcement has been complemented by emphasis on system reform.**

There is a mixed record of success of Lok Ayuktha in different states, which is a reflection of the nature of political support and availability of financial and professional resources. The central government has set up a special commission for redress of public grievances as distinct from the ombudsman. Some public sector undertakings such as the nationalised banks and insurance corporations have set up ombudsmen to resolve complaints. Kerala has appointed an ombudsman for local bodies and other states are following this example. The Andhra Pradesh Government has set up the Commission on People's Empowerment (COPE) under the chairmanship of the former central vigilance commissioner and with representation of civil society to make recommendations on people-oriented administration.

## 3.14 Departmental Enquiries and Enforcing Sanctions

### *Enquiry Rules and Procedures*

Besides prosecution under the Prevention of Corruption Act for corrupt behaviour, departmental enquires can be initiated by individual departments or by the DOPT against regular employees for misconduct and lack of probity. Elaborate provisions are available in the rules relating to various services within the context of constitutional protection against arbitrary dismissal or punishment. The service rules in all states contain special rules and elaborate provisions to initiate disciplinary proceedings for violation of the code of conduct, misappropriation of public money and disobedience.

The disciplinary regulations, often contained in a manual, usually cover many or all of the following areas:

- types of misconduct;
- major and minor punishments;
- suspension;
- different stages of disciplinary proceedings;
- consultation of the PSC or vigilance authority; and
- appeal procedures.

The disciplinary authority is required to consult the UPSC and Central Vigilance Commissioner for Group A and other designated officers before a final decision on punishment is made. The employee has the right of appeal to government or he can file a case before the Central Administrative Tribunal (CAT) or the High Court.

The rules provide for the imposition of the following penalties on a government servant, namely:

**Minor Penalties**

(i) censure;

(ii) withholding of promotion;

(iii) recovery from their pay of the whole or part of any pecuniary loss caused by government by negligence or breach of orders;

(iv) reduction to a lower stage in the time-scale of pay for a period not exceeding three years, without cumulative effect and not adversely affecting pension rights;

(v) withholding increments of pay;

**Major Penalties**

(vi) reduction to a lower stage in the time-scale of pay for a specified period;

(vii) reduction to lower time-scale of pay, grade, post or service which shall ordinarily be a bar to the promotion of the government servant to the time-scale of pay, grade, post or service from which he was reduced;

(viii) compulsory retirement;

(ix) removal from service which shall not be a disqualification for future government employment;

(x) dismissal from service which shall ordinarily be a disqualification for future government employment.

In every case in which the charge of possession of assets disproportionate to known source of income or the charge of acceptance from any person of any gratuity, other than legal remuneration, as a motive or reward for doing or forbearing to do any official act is established, the penalty mentioned in clause (ix) or clause (x) shall be imposed.

A departmental enquiry procedure can be broadly broken down into the following stages:

(i) Preliminary enquiry or investigation, including decision-making on the basis of enquiry/investigation;

(ii) The enquiry proceedings, including charge sheet, reply, conduct of enquiry by the Enquiry Officer and the report of the Enquiry Officer;

(iii) Tentative decision-making on the basis of the report of the Enquiry Officer, including consultation with constitutional and other concerned authorities like the UPSC and the CVC, where necessary;

(iv) Final decision-making and imposition of a penalty or order of exoneration by the disciplinary authority;

(v) Appeal or revision against the penalty imposed by the disciplinary authority.

The CVC supervises the vigilance-related enquiries which are conducted by the officers attached to the CVC. State vigilance commissioners and Lok Ayuktha oversee the enquiries arising out of vigilance matters or complaints sent to them. However, the final decision on imposing punishment is taken by the competent authority as specified in regulations. In Orissa, Uttar Pradesh, Andhra Pradesh and Karnataka, departmental enquiries for officers below the level of Group B are initiated by their departments, while the Personnel Department orders enquiries for higher level officers and the All India Services. DG Vigilance or the Vigilance Commission also refer cases for departmental enquiry in cases where corruption charges cannot be established. States like Andhra Pradesh, Orissa and Uttar Pradesh have established the office of commissioner for departmental enquiries, staffed by senior officers. The departments have the option of referring the conduct of enquiry to the Commissioner for departmental enquiry or to departmental officers. Andrha Pradesh and Tamil Nadu have set up tribunals for enquiries with judicial officers to which vigilance-related cases can be referred. Under Article 320 of the constitution, the PSC is required to be consulted by the state on disciplinary matters affecting employees appointed by the Governor and by other officers working in a civil capacity as specified by the government.

### *Challenges*

The general picture is one of long delays in departmental enquiries, often stretching to more than three years, inefficient conduct of enquiries by departmental officers and the failure of enquiries to result in swift and exemplary punishment for the delinquent officers. The Tamil Nadu Ramanujam Committee of 1998 and the Central Vigilance Commissioner have referred to the low proportion of cases resulting in major punishment and the lack of deterrent effect of departmental enquiries. Departmental enquiries, like other service matters, are agitated before the State Administrative Tribunal or the High Courts often due to infirmities in the charge sheet or the conduct of the enquiry or the failure to follow due process of law such as the furnishing of essential documents. While the innocent employee thus suffers the trauma of enquiry, uncertainty and the injustice of denial of promotion and other rewards, the guilty person is able to prolong the ultimate decision and carry on with his old conduct.

Central and state personnel departments attribute the delays partly to the low priority given by most departments to the processing of disciplinary proceedings, the indifferent preparation of charge sheets, delay in the disposal of interim representations of affected officers and the delays in disposal of references made to the PSC or the Vigilance Commission. There is often a multiplicity of agencies responsible for departmental enquiries, calling attention to the necessity to bring them under the overall oversight of an apex agency like the Vigilance Commission.

### *Reforms*

It is a long held view that the certainty and not the severity of punishment acts as a deterrent to others. In recognition of existing problems, the central government and some states have issued instructions in recent years for the implementation of a number of reforms. They have prescribed definite time limits for each stage of the enquiry with the total time period generally not exceeding six months. Government is acting on the recommendations of the committee set up by the central Ministry of Personnel for reforming the present system, including:

- Rationalising the penalties;

- Distinguishing between administrative lapses and vigilance cases;
- Streamlining the present proceedings and laying down time limits;
- Preparing solid documentation;
- Ensuring the appointment of qualified and motivated enquiry officers working full time;
- Ensuring speedy decisions on the charge sheet and enquiry report;
- Reducing the areas of consultation with the PSC and CVC and the time taken for receiving advice at the stages of initiating the enquiry and imposing punishment;
- Installing computerised systems for effective monitoring of progress;
- Preventing the recurrence of procedural deficiencies pointed out by the courts; and
- Formulation of an administrative law to replace the present rules.

Some states have also begun efforts to streamline their disciplinary procedures. Karnataka has reported good progress in the disposal of cases after the decision to entrust departmental enquiries to retired judges on payment of honoraria. Andhra Pradesh is devising a computerised system for monitoring the progress of enquiries, as well as amendments to rules and procedures.

Demands have been made by experts and political leaders to dilute the provisions of the Constitution, which could be construed as affording excessive protection to civil servants. This demand is born of frustration over many court orders that upset executive decisions to terminate or punish employees. In government's perception, the answer is perhaps not to dilute government job security or to expose potentially corrupt civil servants to public shame without due process, but to install and enforce measures for better management and greater accountability. Managers should be held responsible for weak disciplinary action or inattention to bad performance, and they should be penalised when 'solving' the problem by transferring the non-performers to another department.

## 3.15 Appeals and Redress for Staff

### *Current Machinery*

The executive instructions of different ministries provide the machinery for appeal by individual employees to higher authorities up to the Minister against any executive order relating to pay and allowances, service conditions, transfer, discrimination or work environment. Employees can submit applications for revision or reversal of orders of punishment.

### *Service Litigation*

The central legislation on Central Administrative Tribunals in 1985 opened a new chapter in the sphere of administering justice to aggrieved government servants in service matters. The Act owes its origin to Article 323 of the Constitution. The Act has provided a less expensive and speedy judicial recourse. Government established 17 benches of the Central Administrative Tribunal (CAT) in different regions. CAT'S jurisdiction has been extended beyond central ministries to 49 authorities under the control of government. The chairperson of CAT is assisted by 16 vice-chairpersons and 49 members drawn from civil servants and retired judges. The central law enabled the state governments to set up state tribunals. Eight state governments have established tribunals under the central law, while some states have enacted legislation for setting up administrative tribunals. Appeals against the orders of tribunals lie to the High Court and Supreme Court.

The administrative tribunals are distinguishable from ordinary courts with regard to their jurisdiction (only for service matters) and procedures. They are free from the shackles of many technicalities of ordinary courts and government servants can plead their case personally or through department officers, as well as through lawyers. A nominal fee of only Rs. 50 must be paid by the litigants for filing an application.

Central government and various states have become aware of the high incidence of cases arising from service matters before the central and state administrative tribunals. From the inception of the Central Administrative Tribunal in November 1985 to October 2002, 392,479 cases were received for adjudication, decisions on 31,655 of which are still pending. The majority of cases in which decisions are pending relate to Group C and D employees and casual labour. The causes of action include selection/promotion, recruitment, *ad hoc* appointment/regularisation, disciplinary proceedings, seniority/ confirmation and scale of pay.

### *Proposed Reforms*

Government is acting on a number of useful recommendations for reducing the pendency of cases before the CAT, streamlining procedures followed by CAT benches, computerisation of systems and devising alternate systems for resolution of service disputes. The Government of Andhra Pradesh is taking action on a detailed study on the exogenous and endogenous causes of pendency in the administrative tribunal. It is also installing a computerised system for monitoring service litigation in government departments.

A number of states have asked the central government to abolish the tribunals in the hope that this would reduce the incidence of service litigation. Government is considering amendments to the CAT legislation in response to this request.

Governments themselves are often responsible for generating legal challenges by employees through unnecessary changes in rules or seniority provisions or by failure to make necessary amendments to existing rules. It is clear that service rules should be overhauled in the centre and states, since litigation is encouraged by infirmities in the rules, absence of enabling rules for some cadres and the inclusion of non-core principles in recruitment rules. This realisation has led to serious efforts to update service rules and procedures relating to preparation of seniority lists and panels for promotion.

The present system for redress of employee grievances does not appear to be functioning effectively in many central agencies, and the employees at the cutting edge in dispersed establishments suffer to a considerable extent. Matters of equal concern are the cumbersome procedures for employee grievances and the existence of too many avenues through which administrative actions can be delayed.

It is clear also that a fundamental overhaul of employee grievance procedures is necessary to reduce the number of cases subject to review by administrative tribunals and, in the vast majority of cases, eventually the courts. One alternative under consideration is to consider department level arbitration mechanisms and reduce the need for employee recourse to the courts in respect of seniority, pay and allowances, promotion, transfer and punishment. This could take the form of a 'Disputes Settlement Administrative Authority' as an alternative to the CAT.

With a large workforce dispersed over the entire country, the Ministry of Railways has been implementing a decentralised system of continuous attention to employee grievance with union participation. The central department of the ARPG has set up a staff grievance redress machinery on the lines of public grievance redress in ministries and departments with a staff grievance redress officer in each agency. The ARPG is monitoring the working of the system. It has analysed the sources of employee grievances under different categories and has devised a computer software programme for tracking the receipt and disposal of grievances. The Department has also issued guidelines to various central agencies on ensuring responsive disposal of grievances as well as access for employees to heads of departments at pre-announced times.

## 3.16 Labour Relations and Welfare Joint Consultative Machinery

The basic objectives of the Joint Consultative Machinery (JCM) are to promote harmonious relations between the government and its employees; to secure the greatest measure of co-operation between government as the employer and the general body of employees in matters of common concern, and to increase the efficiency of public services through collaborative endeavour. The aim is to narrow areas of unresolved differences and widen areas of agreement on substantive issues of common concern.

In 1966, central government introduced a scheme for Joint Consultation and Compulsory Arbitration for employees on the lines of the Whitley Councils in the UK. This is a non-statutory and voluntary scheme. The Permanent Negotiating Machinery of Railways predates the JCM. Most states have set up similar joint consultative machinery for government and recognised employee unions.

The scheme for JCM provides for a three tier machinery: the National Council as the apex body presided over by the Cabinet Secretary;

departmental councils at the level of individual ministries and departments, including their attached and subordinate offices; and regional councils to deal mainly with local problems at the level of each field office. Detailed guidelines have been issued for the recognition of unions. The scope of the JCM includes all matters relating to conditions of service and work, welfare of employees and improvement in efficiency and standards of work. However, individual cases are not considered and consultation is limited to matters of general principles in regard to recruitment, promotion and discipline. Government has agreed that the Staff Inspection Unit studies and the proposals of departments for rightsizing would be placed before departmental councils for information.

Under the JCM, there has been continuous interaction with the staff at national and departmental level, besides regular meetings of the Standing Committee of the National Council. Many issues which come up in major ministries such as Railways, Posts and Defence are resolved through negotiations. An important feature of the JCM is the provision for compulsory arbitration in case of any disagreement in the National Council or Departmental Council between the official and employee sides relating to pay and allowances, weekly hours of work and leave of a class or grade of employees. A Board of Arbitration under an independent chairperson, and with a representative each of government and employees, has been set up under the administrative control of the Ministry of Labour. Awards made by the Board are binding on both sides subject to the over-riding authority of Parliament. The Supreme Court has recently declared that government servants do not enjoy the basic right to strike and that available avenues of conciliation should be exhausted before direct action is taken.

### *Staff Welfare*

As the largest single employer in the country, government bears the responsibility of looking after the welfare of employees. Improvements in employees' living and working conditions are expected to enhance morale and efficiency. Women's rest rooms and day care centres for the children of employees are available in a number of places. The DOPT supports various staff welfare measures. It provides grants to resident welfare associations in government colonies. The Central Civil Services Cultural and Sports Board promotes sports and cultural activities in a number of cities. *Grih Kalyan Kendra* (welfare centre) was set up to provide technical and vocational training and to organise opportunities for gainful employment for employees and their family members. It operates in 38 centres in Delhi and other cities. It is conducting a one-year diploma course in software technology for employees. The Central Government Employers Consumer Cooperative Society operates under the name of *Kendriya Bhandar* to provide quality goods to employees at reasonable prices through various outlets.

A number of ministries have set up housing societies for central employees and these societies build and sell houses at reasonable cost in different places. Loans are available for employees for the purchase and construction of houses. The central government health scheme provides medical and hospital facilities for serving and retired employees in different places in return for a small monthly contribution.

# 4 Making Government More Efficient and Removing Constraints

## 4.1 Selecting Appropriate Organisational Structures in Government

### *The Changing Role of Government*

The tenth Five-year Plan pointed out that an important aspect of the redefinition of plan strategy is related to the role of government. The public sector is much less dominant than it used to be in many critical sectors and its relative position is likely to decline further as government ownership in many existing public sector organisations declines to a minority.

This is not to say that government has no role to play, or only a minimalist role, in promoting development. There are many areas, for example the social sectors, where its role will clearly have to increase. There are other areas, for example infrastructure development, where the private sector cannot be expected to make a significant contribution and the role of government may have to be restructured. In others, for example telecommunications, power and ports, the private sector can play a much larger role provided an appropriate policy framework is in place. In all these areas, the role of government in creating and maintaining a modem regulatory system for ensuring a fair deal for consumers, transparency and accountability, and a level playing field is also extremely important.

The huge size of the Council of Ministers in central and state governments has been an important factor in the proliferation of functions, departments and secretaries. The approach suggested by the FCPC and the ERC has provided the basis for the prior options analysis based on whether the function needs to be done at all, or if the government should perform it, and if it should be implemented directly or through other levels or agencies. Continuous efforts are being made to merge and abolish many departments and central agencies in the course of evolving a more compact government structure. Parliament has recently approved a constitutional amendment to restrict the size of the Council of Ministers in central and state governments to 15 per cent of the members in the lower house of the legislature. This will hopefully open the door for the reduction and rationalisation of ministries and departments and the agencies under them. Apart from reduction in the quantum of work due to the rationalisation of functions, government has been implementing measures to improve efficiency and reduce the number of employees required through internal organisational changes and the introduction of technology and modernisation (see Box 4.1).

**_Box 4.1_ Internal Organisational Changes**

**The ongoing steps for organisational improvements in central and state governments are:**

- **A reduction in the number of attached agencies and field offices;**
- **Zero-based audit of schemes and sunset provisions for schemes and staff;**
- **Introduction of officer-oriented system in government;**
- **Delayering and level jumping in decision-making and multi-skilling of employees;**
- **Office automation, reduction of paperwork, change in office systems and file management and eliminating repetitive tasks;**
- **Computerisation.**

### *Challenges Faced by States*

Additional considerations of multi-level governance confront the state governments. One is the trend for the progressive transfer of many centrally sponsored schemes in different sectors to the states as a part of a strategy to redraw the lines of central and state government. The redefinition in the case of states also hinges on the organisational implications of the 73rd and 74rd constitutional amendments for the devolution of functions to elected bodies in rural and urban areas and user management of natural resources and social services.

A number of progressive states have realised that a strategy for redefinition of roles involves both exercises cutting across all departments and directorates to rationalise, eliminate and realign functions, and department level exercises to redefine functional goals, identify and reduce overlaps, and undertake internal rationalisation of functions and delegation of powers. They have divided departments into eight functional groups and set up committees for internal co-ordination within the groups.

### *Separating Policy and Execution*

The organisational pattern of departments and directorates/heads of departments was originally envisaged as a way of separating the secretariat policy-making exercise from the task of implementation and management of field staff, especially in agriculture, forests, education, health and industries. At the same time, departmental enterprises like the Railways provide excellent examples of the separation of policy and execution and the grant of autonomy to zonal and division managers in the areas of personnel and finance. Agencies like RITES under the Railways Ministry are similar to Crown Enterprises in New Zealand and generate surplus from their operations. The Postal Department has separated profit centres like Speed Post into autonomous units within the Ministry. Independent agencies like the National Highways Authority have full authority over the use of budgeted and borrowed funds.

Ministries often set up autonomous agencies with separate boards of management for specific thrust areas. A popular approach to shedding departmental responsibility in the states has been to entrust the execution of works and schemes to arms-length agencies such as corporations and autonomous boards. States like Andhra Pradesh are granting increasing autonomy to individual departments in the flexible use of budgetary allocation, levy of user charges and management of personnel, once the envelope of expenditure and revenues has been agreed in annual budget discussions.

### *Implementation Structures*

Two models of programme or project management are in operation in schemes financed by central government in order to neutralise the problems of departmentalism. Firstly, there are matrix forms of organisation to deal with the problem of inter-departmental co-ordination and delays in implementation. These includes the Kerala model of the NGO-run state campaign for adult literacy; the mission mode of programme management in Madhya Pradesh; the Andhra Pradesh model of the autonomous state implementation society, Andhra Pradesh Prathmik Vidya Parishattu (primary education), to manage district primary education; and the Uttar Pradesh model of state-wide family welfare services through voluntary agencies under the supervision of an autonomous society funded by USAID.

Central government started the trend of setting up technology missions for organising the execution of schemes with time-bound goals such as rural water supply and immunisation. The mission mode entails clarity of objectives and strategies; action within a definite timeframe; an assured budget, fast-track procedures; a committed team of officials; inter-sector effort; collective action; close monitoring; and transparent evaluation. Some states like Madhya Pradesh also set up missions, centring on areas of universal literacy, health and livelihood security in rural areas.

The second organisational solution is the creation of autonomous societies, registered under the Societies Registration Act, for the implementation of major social projects assisted by donor agencies or central ministries. Central government had already set the trend with the agreement with states for the constitution of district rural development agencies to receive and utilise funds for specified activities as well as district societies for various disease control programmes. The objective was to combine the flexibility and innovation of an NGO with the legitimacy and authority of government support.

### *Functional Reviews*

Organisational or functional reviews have been a useful tool in providing an analysis of restructuring options at departmental and agency levels and opportunities for rationalisation. Reviews of the ERC, and the exercises in Orissa, Karnataka and Maharashtra provide excellent models for such reviews, leading to the recasting of functions and ministries in central and state government. The ERC undertook a major exercise for functional review of 36 ministries and departments involving 800,000 employees. Its recommendations envisaged the winding up of some activities together with concerned divisions, privatisation and outsourcing wherever feasible and the restructuring of organisation and staff composition following computerisation and improved work practices. The Karnataka ARC looked at the scope for organising agriculture and forestry on territorial rather than functional lines and of avoiding parallel functioning of specialised cadres in the district with little internal co-ordination. The Orissa review was followed by a zero-based functional audit and the redeployment of redundant staff The reviews were rolled into ongoing exercises for organisational restructuring, sector strategy exercises and the devolution of functions to PRIs.

### *Public Enterprise Reform*

India has 240 central government public sector enterprises and there are 946 state-level public enterprises. India's privatisation programme has evolved over the years.

#### *Box 4.2* Public Enterprise Reform in Andhra Pradesh

Andhra Pradesh began to reform the state public enterprise sector in 1999. A quasi-independent privatisation secretariat and implementation committee were created, and a Cabinet committee was set up to vet public enterprises selected for liquidation, restructuring or privatisation. The procedures for evaluating public enterprise assets, preparing tendering documents for competitive bids, and awarding bids, were set up in the implementation secretariat. The state also established procedures for providing retirement payments to public enterprise employees who would lose their jobs, as well as a social safety net.

Between 1999 and March 2003, Andhra Pradesh successfully liquidated, privatised or restructured 31 public enterprises, ranging from operating sugar factories and fertiliser factories, to agro industry and handicraft corporations. Already Rs. 1750 million in gross proceeds has been realised from the sale of assets. Over the next two years an additional 53 corporations, co-operatives and enterprises with minority government ownership are scheduled for processing.

Several factors have contributed to these achievements, including political support from the top, the creation of an implementation secretariat with a commitment to the programme and technical assistance for building institutional capacity and providing advice. Part of its success comes from putting in place the VRS and social safety net programme to compensate employees for the loss of jobs and assist them in finding alternative employment. As of January 2003, over 18,000 employees in Phase I and II had taken VRS.

A separate department for disinvestment has guided the privatisation of public undertakings by the dilution of equity or strategic sale in consultation with line departments. Central government has sold its controlling stake in some 30 public enterprises, including several industrial enterprises, the former monopoly provider of international telecom and a number of public sector hotels. Many state governments came up with similar policies for reforming public enterprises under their control, privatising or closing public enterprises with a commercial orientation, closing sick public enterprises, and restructuring other public enterprises by the induction of strategic partners or merger/consolidation. Where it is decided to retain public enterprises under state ownership, steps are taken to reform the management and give it greater autonomy.

## 4.2 Corporatisation and Outsourcing

Privatisation, public sector reform and the withdrawal of government from many areas are affecting the administrative structure for policy and implementation in central and state governments. Over the past decade, India has made considerable advances in reducing the state's role in key industry and service sectors, and opening these up to domestic and foreign competition. Public sector units in sectors such as car manufacturing, telecommunications and IT have been privatised. In sectors like telecommunications, banking, insurance and health, which were previously under the exclusive control of public sector monopolies, private companies, both domestic and foreign, have been allowed to operate. Foreign direct investment (FDI) policies were substantially liberalised at an early stage of the reforms. Limits on the permissible share of foreign equity have been liberalised by allowing 100 per cent foreign ownership in a large number of industries and majority ownership in almost all the others.

Corporatisation is seen as a half-way house to privatisation in the overall framework of disinvestment strategy. Central and state governments have converted some manufacturing and service departments into corporations. The departmental enterprise which provided basic telecommunications services in India has been converted into a fully-fledged corporation. Irrigation corporations handle many construction projects for water resources. The entire procurement and distribution system for medicines in Tamil Nadu has been handled successfully over the years by a corporation under the health department.

### *Box 4.3* Areas for Contracting Government Services

**The government's Core Group on AR envisages that contracting in routine operations in government and public enterprises would cover watch and ward/security services, catering services, vehicles and drivers, housekeeping services, travel and ticketing services, processing of medical reimbursement claims, design, construction and maintenance of government buildings and residential colonies, all training activities, operation of telephone system, messenger services, evaluation and monitoring, laboratories, maintenance of railway stations, airports and ports, maintenance of monuments and gardens, postal deliveries, printing, audio-visual publicity, translation, typing and stenography, computer-related services and maintenance of accounts. The Railways have launched an Own-Your-Wagon scheme for investment by rail users.**

**The state governments are following the central example. Gujarat state has enacted a build-operate-transfer or BOT law. Maharashtra is one of the few states to corporatise a major tertiary health facility in Mumbai, having formed a joint venture with more than 50 per cent equity participation from the private sector. Municipal laws have been amended to facilitate outsourcing of services. Maharashtra has franchised the entire operation of computerised registration of documents as well as counter services for citizens in offices of district collector.**

Contracting in cities like Surat, New Bombay, Baroda, Ahmedabad, Vijayawada, Pune, Bangalore, Kochi and Jaipur, covers such operations as meter reading and bill collection for water supply and power, maintenance of streetlights and public taps, maintenance of roads and traffic circles, parks and playgrounds, garbage collection and transport, recovery of taxes and charges, computer services, supplies to nutrition centres and operating welfare outlets. Cities are entrusting to architects the power of issuing commencement certificates for construction and are using professionals and business associations to issue certificates of valuation. Franchising of information technology services is quite common in central and state ministries.

Alternative service delivery has involved a wide range of operators beyond the use of private contractors. Co-operatives spawn a wide range of activities and innovations, including the Operation Flood Programme in dairy development, fertiliser distribution and marketing of agricultural commodities, as agencies of government or independent organisations. Examples of innovative mobilisation of community groups and NGOs are given in another chapter.

Government recognises that various legal and institutional factors restrict the widespread use of contracting or alternative service delivery, even for services regarding which there is no political opposition. There is opposition from vested interests to relinquishing monopoly control. Many political leaders believe that contracting out services might expose poor people to exploitation and make the city or region vulnerable to service disruption. The process requires considerable preparation and careful management, and needs to be kept as transparent as possible. Government is considering amendments to labour laws to minimise the scope for litigation and to widen the areas for contracting out services.

## 4.3 Review of Laws, Regulations and Procedures

### *Review of Administrative Laws*

Central and state governments have recognised the role of legal and regulatory changes in the success of macroeconomic policies and people-friendly administration. The progress of statutory reform has taken place a number of fronts. Firstly, it has been necessary to make changes because of multilateral agreements such as the WTO conventions and agreements on bio-diversity. Secondly, there are changes consequent to liberalisation and reduced state involvement in areas like industry, telecommunications, highways, power, insurance and banking. Thirdly, there are legislative changes related to economic reform and remedying abuses of present laws, such as the repeal of urban land ceiling law and amendment to the foreign exchange regulation law, laws on money laundering, abolition of the Monopolies Commission, procedural changes and amendments to the Essential Commodities Act and Rent Control Act. Fourthly, it was necessary to unify and harmonise statutes and regulations at central and state level to reduce overlap and duplication. An exercise also took place to harmonise the contrasting perspectives of ministries in areas such as environmental control and excise duty. A fifth area was the simplification of existing laws, regulations and procedures, repeal of obsolete laws, reform of laws operating against the weaker sections of society and steps taken to reduce the time and cost of procedures in civil and criminal cases.

### *Box 4.4* Central Commission on Administrative Law

**The Commission was set up by central government in May 1998 to review and advise on the status of administrative law and recommend repeal of or amendments to existing laws and regulations. The Commission made recommendations relating to amendments/changes in the laws, rules, regulations and procedures; repeal of dysfunctional and irrelevant laws; documentation and simplification of laws, subordinate legislation and executive orders. The Commission reviewed over 2500 laws and recommended the repeal of about 1400 laws and amendment of a further 241. It also recommended the enactment of new laws in the emerging areas of international law, cyber laws and environment. Reforms were recommended in the regulatory framework relating to various sectors and many laws affecting the livelihood and access to services for the poor. The Commission added its voice to the reports of other commissions in recommending reforms in civil and criminal procedures and in favour of expanding the system of alternative ways of settling disputes.**

**Government has constituted a Standing Committee under the Chairmanship of the Secretary (Personnel), assisted by the Department of ARPG for monitoring action on the implementation of the report's recommendations. Inter-departmental committees were set up with gas user representation to review cross-cutting themes such as income tax and excise law, cyber law, capital markets, crimes against women, labour law, etc. Most ministries and departments have made suitable amendments/ modifications in the laws and regulations administered by them. 405 laws have been repealed so far. 37 Acts have been amended and bills to amend another 18 Acts are pending in the Parliament.**

The entire law of land acquisition was reviewed to enable speedier acquisition for highways and other infrastructure projects. Procedural laws were amended to bring them in line with current developments such as the acceptance of electronic documents, new forms of apartment ownership and the changing nature of capital markets. It is envisaged that the entire process of approval and issue of permits will be made simpler, more transparent and based on single window systems. The National Informatics Centre has made software available for the computerisation of court procedures and the retrieval of cause lists and court decisions by lawyers and clients.

New laws have been enacted for digital services and e-commerce, regulation of capital markets and dematerialised transactions, money-laundering, overhauling the power sector, insurance regulation, bankruptcy, streamlining company law, competition, fiscal responsibility, electoral reform, copyright and intellectual property rights. Widespread public access has been ensured to all central laws and judgements of Supreme Court.

### *Challenges*

Despite these striking initiatives, external observers believe that it is possible and necessary to quicken the pace of reform in laws which affect disposal of cases, constrain economic and regulatory decision-making and hamper the flow of services to citizens and industry. Procedures for the liquidation of corporations and resolution of cases under labour laws need to be expedited. Regulations and procedures often leave room for subjective interpretation at the lower level and create potential for harassment and corruption, as in the laws relating to land and real estate, labour, environmental clearances and taxation. Multiple approvals are needed at central and state level for many transactions, although delays which result from these have been reduced following the delegation of many powers to the states under environmental and other laws and the consequent move to single window systems.

The most critical issue remains the delay in the resolution of cases. An estimated 25 million cases are pending in different courts and it could take up to 20 years for some cases to be resolved. Owing to government involvement in many areas and micro-level regulation, government is a party to as many as 65 per cent of civil cases. Besides deregulation, government is taking a number of steps such as effective monitoring, devising procedures to reduce unnecessary appeals, reduction of disputes between different levels of the public sector and setting up fast track courts. The recourse to dispute resolution mechanisms such as conciliation, mediation and arbitration can help to reduce the pressure on the judiciary. Government has enacted wide-ranging amendments to the Civil Procedure Code to speed up the resolution of cases. The backlog has fallen considerably in the Supreme Court and some High Courts thanks to the reform of current procedures and computerisation. Some states are following the central lead by initiating steps to build secretariat capacity for monitoring and managing government litigation, to streamline and computerise procedures in tribunals and courts, and to train personnel in legal reform.

## 4.4 Deregulation of Industry and Services

### *Status of Reforms*

The package of second generation reforms following the first phase of delicensing and removal of control has included significant steps for deregulation of different sectors and the effort is continuing. While the regime of licences has been largely dismantled in central government, industrial establishments in some states could still be subject to licensing problems and inspections from many agencies. Central ministries and state governments have set up expert committees with user representation to review rules and regulations and devise ways to make them user-friendly. Independent surveys of small and large industrialists and business across states and cities have been undertaken with the help of industry federations and voluntary agencies. Advisory councils attached to the office of the Prime Minister, individual central ministries and state departments have provided valuable feedback on reforms, Simplification and transparency of the legal and regulatory framework for procurement is considered critical for effective use of public funds and reduced potential for corruption. Central ministries and states are improving the procurement system to meet standards of economy, competition, accountability and honesty. States such as Tamil Nadu and Karnataka have enacted laws for transparency in procurement and public works, while states such as Punjab and Andhra Pradesh have announced their intention to enact such a law. Electronic procurement has been introduced in Andhra Pradesh, Delhi and Tamil Nadu for most departments.

Legal and procedural changes have facilitated quick transfer of assets, such as the repeal of the law relating to sick industries and the introduction and strengthening of bankruptcy and foreclosure laws. The recently enacted amendments to the Companies Act should help improve the bankruptcy framework. The recently passed law on the enforcement of creditors' rights will help the process of industrial restructuring, unlocking resources tied up in non-performing

### *Box 4.5* Steps Towards Deregulation

- Greater flow of information to the public on regulations, procedures and changes in policy through White Papers and information on the internet;
- Enactment of enabling laws for industrial facilitation and enabling a single inspector to perform inspections for multiple departments at times convenient to the client;
- Re-engineering all procedures, simplification of registration for industry and business, virtual submission of forms, single window systems for all approvals and clearances under different laws and adoption of a common format for multi-agency approvals;
- Computerised counters in field offices such as district industry centres for registration, information and facilitation, backed by delegation of authority to local officers;
- Delegation of powers under central laws for environmental and other clearances to state agencies and district officers;
- Removal of licensing, trading and movement controls for most agricultural commodities;
- Relaxation of restrictions under labour laws for the hiring and separation of workers;
- Extending validity of statutory permits, providing for automatic approvals after the expiry of stipulated period, permitting self-certification and permitting alternate agencies for issue of permits and valuation certificates;
- Notification of a Common Building Code to reduce the number of approvals required for site, building plans and layout for industries in industrial townships or outside;
- Abolition of unnecessary committees and commissions under different laws;
- Publication of a single-source book for businesses informing them of the change in procedures and policies and time limits for transactions;
- Promotion of customer-friendly procedures in banks and financial institutions;
- Resolution of disputes through departmental ombudsmen, strengthening systems for tracking and resolving grievances and speedy steps to penalise fraud by market operators;
- Increasing use of information technology for various transactions and installation of single portals for industry with downloadable forms.

enterprises for more productive use. Power sector reforms are now widely accepted as having contributed to improved business performance. The reform relating to the project cycle in government will ensure that sources of delay such as environment and forest clearances and relocation are addressed before detailed project reports are formally approved and public money spent.

State governments seek to address the difficulties of entrepreneurs at the three levels of entry, implementation and operation by necessary changes in rules under different Acts. Efforts are being developed in Andhra Pradesh to evolve a public relations/outreach strategy for the 29 departments involved in industrial and commercial clearances, as well as to improve procedures for the redress of grievances.

### *Regulatory Bodies*

Together with liberalisation and increasing privatisation of utilities, it has become imperative to lay down the rules and institutional framework to ensure that there is a level playing field for public and private providers, and the safeguard the protection of consumers and fixing of tariffs. Central government has enacted legislation to set up independent regulatory authorities in telecommunications, electricity, ports and insurance. Electricity regulatory authorities operate at the state level as well. The authorities decide disputes among providers, set tariffs and operate with complete transparency. Government no longer combines the roles of licensing, regulation, direct operation of utilities and tariff fixing. Government's role is now limited to direct operation through public undertakings in competition with other providers licensed by the regulator. The Reserve Bank of India continues to regulate nationalised and private banks and financial institutions. The Securities and Exchange Board of India has distinguished itself by various measures to ensure the transparency of operations, investor protection and prompt settlement in the stock exchange. There is a demand for regulatory authorities in water supply, transport and other state level services.

There was some initial confusion about the division of jurisdiction of the regulator and the government and the responsibility for establishing ground rules for competition and tariff fixation; but ambiguity is being resolved with greater understanding of market forces, public pressure and co-operation of operators. The regulatory authorities have already established considerable credibility in the minds of the public and business and have encouraged an increasing flow of investment in different areas of infrastructure. The increasing role of these authorities has tilted the balance of regulation away from ministries and has ensured more stable policies free from the political cycle. There are several reasons why changing procedures are figuring prominently in any programme of administrative reform and modernisation in states with relatively less capacity. First and foremost, these changes are easier to implement than more complex administrative reforms. Second, simplification of procedures is less threatening to those in authority and less daunting to officers inured to complex systems in contrast to some of the difficult administrative reforms attempted elsewhere. Procedural reforms can in fact be used as short cuts to demonstrate 'quick wins' while the ground is being prepared for the more difficult administrative reforms.

## 4.5 Modernisation of Offices, Record Management and Work Practices

Deregulation was initially limited to business and industry and inadequate attention was given to decision-making systems within government. Expert committees and state commissions have pointed out that the functioning of the Secretariat is hampered by lack of inter-departmental co-ordination, file pendency, lack of delegation of powers to departments and field offices, adherence to outdated procedures, inadequate use of information technology and the low level of automation and modern equipment. Elaborate office systems and procedures generated unnecessary file work, reports and returns. Employees, especially those in field offices, were constrained by inadequate working space, amenities, inappropriate furniture and lack of modern equipment.

### *Effecting Improvements in Secretariat Procedure*

Government has taken several measures to change the traditional image of government offices in tune with the goal of effective and responsive administration. The Department of ARPG constituted four committees on procedural reforms in July, 2000: reforms in recruitment rules; appointment to senior positions; vigilance procedures; and service litigation. They were all requested to make recommendations relating to simplification of rules and procedures, elimination of steps in decision-making, including statutory references to various bodies and framing suitable legislation to pre-empt judicial interventions in certain matters. Government has acted on the recommendations of these four committees.

### *Box 4.6* Officer-oriented Secretariat System

**Efforts to convert the central secretariat into a desk officer system began in 1973 and led to the abolition of sections and unnecessary supporting staff, a reduction of the number of levels by at least two, a reduced accent on noting and increased stress on oral communication. The efforts helped to foster greater participation and commitment to organisational goals among officers.**

**Under the desk officer system, each desk was given a defined area and placed under an under-secretary or section officer who was helped by an assistant and section libraries of files. There are 1816 sections and 427 desks in the central secretariat. It is now realised that the desk officer system is more suited to certain functions than others. New departments, such as information technology, have adopted officer-oriented systems from the start. The officer-oriented systems have been accompanied by steps to create a multi-skilled position of executive assistant to replace the posts of clerks and assistants. The long-term goal is that the desk officer system, supported by a computerised environment, an institutional memory and a revised record management system will be extended to all areas of administration.**

**A number of state governments have implemented similar measures. Maharashtra has a long tradition of desk officer system operating in many departments, including personnel and finance.**

Central government undertook revision of the Central Secretariat Manual of Office Procedure (CSMOP), civil service rules and financial rules to convert the Secretariat into an efficient and responsive organ of government. Significant moves have been made to delegate financial powers to departments and field offices and for the further delegation to offices under heads of departments. Powers relating to decisions on investments under plan and non-plan heads have been substantially delegated to committees under the departmental secretary. Screening committees under the departmental secretary, and with the representation of officers from finance and personnel, are competent to decide on the revival of vacant posts and annual recruitment plans subject to guidelines. The CSMOP contains useful provisions to reduce the time taken to resolve the majority of repetitive cases by using standard process sheets and the manual of housekeeping jobs. The ISTM provides training for secretariat officers and personal assistants of officers in the effective use of the manual and computerised systems.

The manuals of office procedure also deal with responsive and speedy communication to members of Parliament and the legislature and the general public, with time limits and penalties for delay. Guidelines for the improvement of the quality of services rendered through the telephones in public offices were issued in January 2000. The compendium of addresses of central ministries and departments and their attached/subordinate offices/PSUs/autonomous bodies is periodically updated and issued to facilitate inter-office correspondence and to inform the public. Each ministry and department prepares, and places before Parliament, annual action plans, divided into monthly components, which clearly specify measurable targets for each functional unit in the department. The ARPG regularly monitors the compliance of procedures laid down in the CSMOP by conducting interactive management studies of various ministries and departments and state governments and follows up the implementation of the recommendations.

### *Restructuring Office Systems*

Restructuring office systems in central offices has involved a variety of steps, including:

- Fixing accountability for delays in decision-making and responding to representations from clients and citizens;
- Reducing unnecessary movement of files within and across departments;
- Fixing the level of disposal for each category, minimising levels of disposal and ensuring that no paper is seen by more then three levels at any one time;
- Clear demarcation of work among branches and heads of departments;
- Reducing the number of files with various offices at any given time;
- Preventing time wasting in locating files and gaining access to information about schemes and activities in other departments;

- Use of a single file system to avoid delay in decisions on matters that are referred by the non-secretariat organisations to the department on approval of schemes, funds, purchases and personnel;
- Improving record management practices and the progressive introduction of digitised systems;
- Freeing officers from routine maintenance of records and eliminating repetitive tasks;
- Improved internal communication across the hierarchy and between departments;
- Electronically Supported Office Procedures and System;
- Fixing time limits for different types of cases and instituting the practice of presumed approval for pendency beyond a reasonable period;
- Delegation of powers.

A number of state governments are effecting similar reforms, often with the help of state ARCs. The ARPG has been providing assistance to states through seminars, interactive studies and training. These steps go along with efforts to raise productivity by improved work environment, office and seating layout and better amenities for employees and the client population. The ARPG has collaborated with the Quality Division of the Confederation of Indian Industries (CII) to introduce TQM practices in departments. Mumbai Municipal Corporation has set up a state of the art tracking system for all papers and grievances at ward level. In a number of divisional offices in states, all the branches are connected by a local area network, with terminals available on the table of all the desks linked by a modern seating plan and neat arrangements for storing records.

The Andhra Pradesh Government has introduced the Secretariat Knowledge and Information Management System (SKIMS), now called *Smartgov* with the aim of improving the management of information and knowledge within the secretariat through a computerised process. The movement and tracking of files can be monitored by managers online. The system will be integrated with the departmental and central record room to enable scanning of records. The system also provides access of employees to leave and service records except for confidential matters and the use of e-mail for all internal communication. The paperless system has so far been introduced in five departments and will be fully scaled up in the entire secretariat by the end of 2004. Andhra Pradesh Technical Services is assisting all state agencies to introduce a similar file tracking and disposal system.

### *Box 4.7* Simplification of Government Forms

**The guidelines issued by the ARPG envisage:**

- **A provision for counter file/acknowledgment should be made in the form itself so that the customer is able to establish that he/she has filed an application before the concerned authority on due date;**
- **The forms prescribed for making an application should contain adequate space to accommodate the information to be filled in;**
- **It should be stipulated in the form itself that the documents mentioned in the application form are only required;**
- **The form should be examined on the spot and the customer advised regarding deficiencies then and there;**
- **The choices to the customer on submission of documents should be clearly indicated in the form itself so that there is no scope for harassment;**
- **In respect of services for which a long queue exists, the customer should be informed every year where he stands vis-a-vis other customers;**
- **Organisations should use the latest information technology to provide any information or gauge for redress of public grievances. The organisations should examine their working days and working hours in relation to customer convenience.**

### *Modernisation and Office Automation*

A scheme for the modernisation of government offices was launched in 1987–88 to provide assistance to various ministries and departments in modernising the functioning of operational areas, including the improvement of the work environment through:

- Functional layouts;
- The creation of open offices to facilitate better supervision;
- Redress of public grievances and better service to the public;

- More efficient management of data through reduction in paper work by using modem aids;
- Cost and space effective record management.

The scheme provides for setting up a model office. A section or unit within the office is taken up for development into a model unit. This unit, in turn, acts as a model for others to emulate over a period of time. Proposals for fax machines, isographs, EPABX, photocopiers, paper shredders, overhead projector, slide projects, a video projection system, etc. are considered subject to the guidelines. Many departments and offices have improved their functional layouts leading to optimum use of office space and have begun to use modern aids to efficient performance and record management.

***Record Management***

Arrangements for the proper classification, storage, preservation and retrieval of records are vital for efficient functioning of the secretariat and for prompt decision-making. The enactment of laws for freedom of information has placed responsibility on all government offices to ensure the proper classification and prompt retrieval of records to enable timely response to demands for information from the public. The Maharashtra legislation on the right to information provides for a Records Commission to advise the government on the management and classification of records for the purpose of easy release of information to the people.

Central Government has enacted the Public Records Act and has set up a national agency to ensure that proper attention is given to the preservation of historic and other records and the training of functionaries in record management. Detailed guidelines have been issued by the ARPG and the National Archives for the classification of records, consignment of files to the record room, preservation of records, periodic review of consigned records and for their prompt retrieval. Assistance has been provided to many departments for modernising the record rooms. Special measures have been taken to ensure appropriate records management through declassification and computerisation of records and microfilming with the help of the National Archives of India. It is proposed to automate record management progressively and support the sharing of such records across departments.

Many offices face problems of inadequate space and inefficient management of records. Innovative approaches by many field officers are making a change in spite of resource constraints. In the offices under the Commissioner (Maharashtra state), the record assistant is able to retrieve details of any record in a few minutes (as compared to months before the introduction of the new system) given only the name of the applicant or the subject and the village. The reforms in record management and computerisation have brought about a tremendous saving in time for people seeking records for various purposes and have led to a reduction in the time taken for litigation and proof of title.

### *Challenges*

The Office Procedure Manual is only as useful and effective in so far as it is understood and sincerely implemented by all employees. The emphasis of government is on on- and off-the-job training, as well as committed support of the secretary or head of department. The effectiveness of the steps for simplifying procedures and decision-making processes, to the extent they impact on the public and business, are periodically assessed by user surveys related to the Citizen's Charter. It is critical to project apparently isolated measures such as the desk officer system, single file system or computerised file movement as elements of an integrated package for improving efficiency, hastening decision making within and across levels of government, emphasising the lead role of the secretary/head of department and transforming the processes of policy-making. As a considerable proportion of internal decisions on files relate to service matters and employee benefits, the employees stand to gain equally from productivity improvements and speedier processes.

## 4.6 Supporting Innovation

### *Involving Employees*

Officers and staff have been asked to promote a new work culture by giving more importance to results rather than procedures, and by looking at requests from the members of the public from the users' point of view and not solely from the point of view of what might be administratively convenient.

An award scheme is being implemented by the ARPG from 1998–99 for central government employees as well as members of the public to elicit innovative and practical suggestions for improving the quality of public services and making them more customer friendly. This scheme has been revamped as 'National Award Scheme 2001'. Suggestions that can lead to financial savings through reduction of manpower and material or that can enhance efficiency and productivity through procedural improvements and reduced paper work/time taken or increase public satisfaction in government offices are rewarded. Under the scheme, awards are also given to outstanding central government operational staff for their services .

***Supporting Innovation***

Apart from the award scheme for suggestions, the ARPG has been encouraging innovations in different fields of administrative reform in central and state ministries. It has hosted a website for the best practices. The department has also drawn up a scheme for providing financial support to the state governments for documentation of best practices in administrative reform and citizen-friendly practices, with a view to ensure their replication in other states.

The Innovations Award programme is a major component of the government's broader strategy to engage and challenge the prevailing public scepticism about government's ability to respond to important social problems and adapt to changing circumstances. The department calls for submissions from all public agencies on innovations in administration and service delivery. The outstanding innovations are short-listed and sponsored for participation in international competitions such as those arranged by the Commonwealth Association for Public Administration and Management (CAPAM). Indian innovations have received the first or second prize in the last few years in various international events. The successful entries included an education guarantee scheme in Madhya Pradesh; Trichy community police; and *Bhoomi,* or computerisation of land records, in Karnataka. This success has encouraged many field officers to excel in their work and document their experiences. The department is sponsoring the cascading of innovative programmes in other Commonwealth programmes by Indian public agencies with the help of CAPAM.

> ***Box 4.8* Institutional Excellence**
>
> **The ARPG is utilising a technical assistance grant from the World Bank to develop an award scheme for institutional excellence in public service delivery. The design of the scheme will be based on the documentation of internal work processes and code of practice, evaluation of operations, development of quality management system, mechanisms for seeking client feedback, understanding the experience of selected organisations. The scheme will develop criteria for selection, procedures to be adopted for ascertaining the eligibility, benchmarking and standardising of evaluation/assessment for comparison and the manner of adjudication.**

A number of state governments are engaged in similar steps to recognise and reward excellence at organisational individual level. Andhra Pradesh is proceeding systematically to devise performance measures for urban and local bodies such as revenue collection, delivery of services and managerial improvements, and then rate the local bodies by independent experts. Successful local bodies and office bearers are given awards and access to public funds. Individual excellence will be rated on the basis of the online performance indicators system and monthly reports by functionaries.

Innovations extend to resource mobilisation and infrastructure development. The concept of bidding for funds on the basis of innovative approaches to public-private partnership or taxation is built into the loans and grants made available to water supply authorities and city agencies by Maharashtra and Karnataka Government as also an ongoing external aid project called the FIRE. Venture funding for innovations is available from national financial institutions like HUDCO. Private foundations such as the National Foundation of India and the Ford Foundation have assisted a programme, removed from government, for commending, awarding and seeding community-government partnerships and local initiatives.

## 4.7 Improving Fiscal Management

Fiscal reforms have been undertaken to ensure a phased reduction in the primary and revenue deficits of the centre and state governments and to reallocate expenditure toward more productive uses. The proposals for policy reforms cover four key areas: (a) tax reform; (b) subsidy reduction; (c) financial policy; and (d) better expenditure management and increased financial accountability. The main reform goal was, therefore, not just to make fiscal savings, but to achieve higher growth in different sectors by shifting central expenditures away from wages and subsidies towards poverty reduction, health, education and productivity-enhancing investments, including agriculture, irrigation, infrastructure, research and extension. At the same time, fiscal reform has been seen as part of a broader programme for revitalising government, accelerating growth and reducing poverty. Tax reform is also a governance issue with the twin objective of reducing compliance costs and improving compliance through more responsive delivery and transparency.

### *Performance and Reform-based Transfers*

Under constitutional provisions, there is an arrangement for tax sharing and transfer of resources from central government to states and union territories based on recommendations of the Finance Commissions every five years. The Twelfth Finance Commission is now holding discussions with all stakeholders. The volume of centre-to-states transfers is based on criteria such as population, per capita income and level of backwardness, but transfers linked to reform and performance are being expanded. In this regard, the creation of the Fiscal Reforms Facility (FRF), following the recommendation of the Eleventh Finance Commission, and the central support under the Accelerated Power Development and Reform Programme for the power sector are steps in the right direction. The FRF provides grant funding for states, which reduces their revenue deficit as a ratio of revenue receipts.

The FRF has had a significant impact on state performance First, it has required states to draw up Medium-term Fiscal Restructuring Plans (MTFRPs) which, for the first time, have placed fiscal policy at state level in a medium-term strategic framework. Second, the borrowing levels agreed on under the MTFRPs are in the nature of global borrowing caps, and have thus helped central government to begin the process of disciplining state borrowing in an environment characterised by multiple borrowing windows. The central Finance Ministry and the Reserve Bank of India have been striving to prevent states from circumventing central controls on budgetary borrowing through the use of off-budget special purpose vehicles.

Centrally sponsored schemes under different ministries are designed to achieve certain national goals like poverty alleviation, universal literacy and minimum standards of infrastructure. However, the schemes have proliferated and created problems of budgetary rigidity, duplication and inadequate monitoring. In order to cope with this problem, the Planning Commission has been working with ministries to consolidate the schemes into compact groups and encourage them to follow a cafeteria approach with flexibility for the states to run schemes in health, agriculture and other sectors according to their needs and priorities.

**_Box 4.9_ Fiscal Responsibility**

**Central government has set a model for states by enacting the Fiscal Responsibility Act to maintain a cap on fiscal deficit and practice responsible fiscal management. Karnataka and Kerala have passed similar legislation and some other states are drafting a new law. Many states have published White Papers on state finances to reveal to the public the nature and cause of fiscal crisis and the measures needed to deal with it. The central government is encouraging states to formulate and publish State Financial Accountability Assessments to set out a road map for a sound financial accountability framework and practices. Andrha Pradesh has published reports on the impact of expenditure in many key sectors. Government has initiated a culture of transparency through better disclosure of financial information.**

### *Public Consultation and Budget Analysis*

As a part of the commitment to greater accountability in the use of public funds, central and state governments are increasingly making the budget document transparent and based on consultation with all the stakeholders. There is an extensive process of pre-budget consultations with different interest groups in central government. State governments such as Andhra Pradesh have started circulating the major budget proposals, except for revenue measures, to elicit public comment, and the final document reflects the results of consultation. Maharashtra Government is proposing to set up an independent agency composed of civil society representatives to provide feedback on the impact of public expenditure and public expectations, to guide the budget process.

### *Box 4.10* Budget Analysis by Civil Society

**Independent review of government budgets by NGOs in India is comparatively recent, as budget analysis has been confined to expert agencies, financial experts and the media. Activists like the National Institute of Budget Advocacy, DISHA in Gujarat and Vidhayak Sansad in Maharashtra soon realised that the focus on the budget was a powerful way of understanding the government's priorities, and monitoring whether commitments on the allocation of funds for programmes benefiting poor and marginalised groups are turned into reality on the ground. The analysis also helped to demystify the budgetary exercise, and expose waste and misallocation of resources. Simple booklets in local languages and English have been published by voluntary agencies in a number of states to stimulate debate by legislators, media and the public on the content and failings of the central and state budgets.**

**The PROOF (Public Record of Operations and Finance) campaign in Bangalore aims at obtaining quarterly financial statements from the government, developing performance indicators to characterise municipal undertakings across the city and initiating public discussions.**

The work of the NGO centres for budget analysis has coincided with the advocacy interests of diverse groups, be they social audit or greater allocation of funds for schemes benefiting the poor. A leading example of the use of budget analysis to increase transparency is the campaign of Mazdur Kisan Sakti Sanghatan (MKSS) in Rajasthan, a citizen group, for the right to information and to see public expenditure records.

The growth of the budget analysis movement in India augurs well for citizen-led budget analysis, much in the manner of the Centre for Budget Priorities and Analysis in the USA and similar agencies in countries like South Africa and Brazil. Kerala state has blazed a trail through exercises in participatory budgeting for development at panchayat, block and district levels and has equipped citizen groups for the task by providing trained resource persons. Partnerships of civil society and public agencies in Bangalore (Karnataka) and some cities in Kerala are extending the exercise to city wards. These exercises bring the element of active citizenship into play in discussions of public expenditure and the priority needs of citizens.

# 5 Accountable and Citizen-centred Government

## 5.1 Accountable and Citizen-friendly Government

Central and state governments increasingly advocate demand-driven approaches to problems of governance through citizen action, increased accountability of public agencies and responsiveness of government agencies to citizen-led initiatives. They wish to ensure an honest, transparent and people-centred government at all levels, thus restoring people's confidence in administration.

The conference statement of chief ministers in May 1997 endorsed measures for: a) making administration accountable and people-friendly; b) ensuring transparency and right to information; and c) improving the performance and integrity of the civil service. This conference was followed by various initiatives at central and state level. Elements of citizen-centred administration in central and state governments under the present government include:

- Formulation and credible implementation of citizen's charters;
- Speedy and effective redress of public grievances;
- Simplification of rules and regulations;
- Decentralisation and partnerships with NGOs and the private sector;
- Easy and widespread access to information on government schemes and procedures and computerised access of land records (such as the *Bhoomi* in Karnataka);
- Facilitation of transactions with public agencies through computerised counter services or virtual sites;
- Reducing the life cycle time of statutory licences, validation and

permits, thus reducing the social and transaction costs of citizens and government;

- Agreeing on key principles and practices, including TQM and a certification process;
- Opportunities for consultation and participation in budgeting, service delivery and resource allocation;
- Documentation and dissemination of good practices within and across states.

There are many examples of government initiatives to ensure responsive delivery of services to the people. Many initiatives are still not institutionalised and pilot projects are being scaled up. The initiatives include:

- State-wide programmes to take administration to the people, such as the *Janmabhoomi* scheme in Andhra Pradesh and 'government at your doors' in Maharashtra;
- State-sponsored initiatives for greater transparency and social audit, such as the works under the Swarnajayanti village prosperity scheme being subjected to audit by *Gram sabha*;
- Steps for participatory management of natural resources, such as watershed development, use of water sources and joint forest management, as well as locally managed services like education, health and basic services;
- Community-based urban basic services and slum upgrading;
- The people's campaign for planning in Kerala and similar initiatives for the empowerment of local bodies and building of people's capacities to function as genuine agents of local development;
- Electronic governance for open and accessible administration;
- Various types of partnerships between public agencies and local government, and civil society and the private sector.

There are schemes with a high political profile and administrative resources to deal with grievances and local demands on the ground. They include Andhra Pradesh (*Janmabhoomi* and *Prajalu Vaddaku Palana*), Assam (*Raijor Padulit Raijor Sarkar*), Haryana (*Sarkar Apke Dwar*), Madhya Pradesh (*Gram Sampark Abhiyan*), Maharashtra

(People's Sovereignty-Day and Headquarters Day), Rajasthan (*Prashasan Gaon ke Sang*) and Tamil Nadu (*Manu Veedhi Thittam*). Such schemes provide the basis for the development of responsive employee attitudes.

## 5.2 Transparency and Access to Information

### *Freedom of Information Laws and Transparency in Administration*

There is a political consensus and popular demand for greater transparency in the functioning of government and public bodies, as this will make democracy and participation meaningful and reduce the scope for corruption. Government agencies are devising measures for widespread and easy access to all information relating to schemes, procedures, performance and decisions of public bodies, except to the extent specifically excluded by law.

Central government appointed a working group in 1997 under the chairmanship of H.D. Shourie, an eminent activist, to formulate a legal framework for freedom of information. The acceptance of the report was followed by a flurry of efforts by central and state governments to enact laws for right to information. The central Freedom of Information Act became the law of the land in January 2003. Government is publishing detailed rules to make the law operational. Besides the legislature, judiciary, government departments and agencies, the law also extends to public sector units and agencies which are substantially funded and controlled by government. Meanwhile, a number of states such as Tamil Nadu, Maharashtra, Karnataka, Goa, Delhi and Rajasthan have enacted their own laws for freedom of information. Kerala has amended its Local Government Act to provide for right to information at the local level. Other states will implement the central law.

Requests for information are to be either accepted or rejected within 30 days of being received, with a shorter period for information affecting the life and liberty of individuals. The applicant has an opportunity to appeal against denial of information at two levels. The rules provide for a schedule of fees for different types of information, the appeal process and the procedures to be followed by information officers. Some state laws provide for the levy of a penalty on officials for furnishing wrong information or for deliberate delay, while the central government envisages proceeding under civil service rules against the concerned officer for misconduct. The Maharashtra Act has a number of progressive features such as the establishment of an advisory council for monitoring the functioning of the legislation and a commission for record management related to the release of information.

**_Box 5.1_ Legal Scheme for Freedom of Information**

**The legal scheme requires public authorities firstly to catalogue and index their records; to publish details concerning their procedures, functions and facilities; to release all relevant facts while announcing a decision or policy; and to inform the public of any likely consequences before initiating or allowing a particular project to proceed. Secondly, all citizens have the right to demand and receive information in written or electronic form within a stipulated period from public information officers in public authorities, except for information specifically excluded under the Act. The exemptions relate to information adversely affecting sovereignty, integrity and public security, public safety and order, progress of criminal investigations, centre-state relations, Cabinet discussions, legislative or judicial privilege, trade or commercial secrets and matters affecting individual privacy. The central law provides for the exemption of notified intelligence and security agencies.**

As the experience of central and state governments shows, mere enactment of legislation is not enough to secure people's entitlement to information if departmental rules and attitudes are not amended and record management is not improved. The climate created by provisions in conduct rules and the fear of prosecution under the Official Secrets Act constrained many civil servants in their efforts to disclose even non-confidential information. Government has already declared that the Official Secrets Act will be modified to the extent of the provisions under the Freedom of Information law. The rules relating to classification of records will be amended with specific regard to the nature of operations of each department. Central and state governments have initiated steps to amend all relevant laws to remove provisions contrary to the intent of the law. Action has been taken to amend Civil Service Conduct Rules and secretariat manuals to conform to the new law.

The public authorities have been advised to make adequate provision and develop procedures to catalogue and index their records in order to ensure that requests for information are speedily processed. Government has issued instructions to all agencies controlled or funded by it to track compliance with the provisions relating to voluntary disclosure, train information officers to respond to public requests for information and publicise the provisions of the Act in ways that can be easily understood by the general public. Given the traditional neglect of record management in several Indian states, government recognises the importance of improved storage (along with computerisation) of records in order to facilitate access to indexed information. Central and state training institutions are providing training in the provisions and details of implementation of the Freedom of Information law to officials.

Government is involving civil society in evaluating how the legislation is working and in building administrative capacity for compliance. The Public Affairs Agency, Bangalore, has issued a report card on the implementation of the law by various state agencies. The Delhi government has benefited from setting up a commission with representatives from government, civil society and business to monitor implementation, publicly report on progress, and serve as an institutional advocate for greater access to information. Some training programmes are facilitated by voluntary agencies such as the Commonwealth Human Rights Initiative. Some states have commenced distance learning training for village panchayat members in freedom of information.

### *Facilitation and Access to Information in Public Offices*

An integral aspect of administrative reforms is speedy and easy public access to information on the services and activities of government and the development of appropriate processes in different departments to enable this access. The information to be made available *suo moto* will be of a general nature, such as the material provided in the *Economic Survey* and White Papers relating to all departments and government activities, development expenditure, budgets and policies. It is also department-specific, such as procedures for permits and approvals, information on procurement and public works, criteria for selection of beneficiaries under government and financial institutions, assessment and levy of taxes and fees, personnel information and the rights of arrested and detained persons. Instructions have been issued to establish accountability and control of *Gram sabhas* over panchayats in respect of construction work and various government programmes. In Rajasthan state, all citizens have been empowered to inspect and take notes from the muster rolls and other records kept in panchayat raj institutions.

The Government of Andhra Pradesh has devised innovative software for providing continuously updated and decentralised information on the status and expenditure of a state-wide programme of food for works. Interactive information portals on the internet have been developed by several central ministries, public enterprises and many states although the quality and breadth of information varies considerably. The central portals of Andhra Pradesh and Delhi provide considerable information to citizens free of charge. Citizen's charters are an alternative means of providing relevant information provided they are well-drafted. Virtual interactive systems of high quality have been developed by a number of district collectors and municipal commissioners in places like Thane, Vishakapatnam and Vijayawada.

Transparency in fiscal policies and the budget is being extended through fiscal transparency laws in central government and some states. Many states have issued White Papers on the state fnances. Tamil Nadu and Karnataka have enacted laws for transparency in tenders and procurement, while a number of states have notified rules to make the process transparent.

### *Integrated Citizen Centres*

Starting with industry, central and state governments have been making efforts since the early 1990s to develop a computerised mechanism to provide information, handle complaints and facilitate transactions at a single point in public offices. The central government has installed information and facilitation counters for the public in 93 ministries and attached offices outside the security zone. These centres provide information and assistance on public schemes and the procedures of the relevant organisation, as well as acknowledgment and status report on applications and grievances. Information is disseminated through brochures, booklets and display boards and through telephone enquiry. A number of central departments such as the Department of Telecommunications and Passport Organisation have set up computerised customer service centres. Evaluation of these counters has shown that the successful functioning of these centres involves: a) process engineering to link different units within an office as well as integrate related offices to enable information-on-tap for the counter staff; b) delegation of powers to personnel at the counter; and c) establishment of computerised networks within and across offices with customised software.

It is proposed to set up multi-utility centres of central and state governments to provide certain value-added services to citizens through one-stop, non-stop shops (OSNSS). Services such as payment of telephone bills, applying for a telephone connection, filing income tax returns, submitting passport applications, making airline and railway bookings, making use of postal services, applying for school, college and university admissions, etc. will be provided through these OSNSS.

### *Box 5.2* Integrated Citizen Centres

**Many state governments have set up information and transaction centres, providing a single or multiple services, and covering a single department or a functional agency or a local body. Services such as payment of electricity bills, supply of ration cards, registration of vehicles, issue of driving licences, filing in a First Information Report (FIR), obtaining birth, death and caste certificates, issue of land holding certificates, etc. will be provided by these centres. The Andhra Pradesh Government launched a project of this nature called e-Seva in a number of cities in 2001. Having covered all urban areas, e-Seva is being extended in a modified form to rural areas.**

**An excellent example of an integrated citizen one-stop service centre open seven days a week is to be found in the FRIENDS project in Thiruvananthapuram, Kerala, which provides over 17 different services on behalf of state and local agencies. The *Lok Mitra* in Rajasthan is the flagship project of Rajasthan. The *Bhoomi* project in Karnataka is an outstanding example of a state-wide effort to issue certificates of land records across the counter and to effect changes in title on the computer. *Gyandoot* in Madhya Pradesh is a unique example of an information and facilitation centre being operated by trained unemployed youth to provide various services to the rural population, including permits from government offices for a modest fee.**

Central Government proposes to support initiatives similar to e-Seva on a pilot basis in selected states. Where possible, the central and state multi-service centres will be integrated for seamless delivery of services to the citizens. Integrated centres could emerge also in respect of multiple services and transactions in municipalities (such as the Dahisar ward centre in Mumbai, centres operated by Vishakapatnam, Guntur and Vijayawada) or centres focusing on the needs of farmers in Maharashtra and Madhya Pradesh (the Wama wired villages and Gyandut), the centres in the office of collectors in Maharashtra, Gujarat and Andhra Pradesh) and the transport offices in Andhra Pradesh. Such centres could be operated by voluntary agencies as in the case of the Swaminathan Foundation in Pondicherry for meeting the all the needs of farmers. The outposts for the office-based centres would be in the form of kiosks to enable easy accessibility for people in remote areas and large cities. The kiosks are being franchised to privatise the sector, as seen in the example of Madhya Pradesh and other states. The Maharashtra experiment with registration of documents and the SETU Citizen Centres in offices of district collectors represent a model of public-private partnership with zero capital investment by the state government. The private party is able to recover the cost of hardware and supporting staff entirely from value-added services like advertisement boards, photocopying and fax services, train and bus reservations, payment of insurance premiums and credit card bills.

## 5.3 Redressing Grievances of the Public and Employees

### *Activities of the Central Department of ARPG*

The Department of ARPG is the chief co-ordination agency of central government for redress of public grievances arising from the work of central departments and organisations. The strategy adopted in the sphere of public grievances has four important aspects:

- To set up or strengthen the grievance redress machinery in various organisations and to evaluate its effectiveness;
- To concentrate more on the identification of systemic deficiencies that give rise to complaints rather than on individual complaints;
- To enlist the co-operation and support of voluntary agencies to supplement governmental efforts in the sphere of public grievances;

- To utilise the media to pass on information on various innovative measures taken by government and to create awareness among the people about their rights and privileges and the services, including grievance redress arrangements, available to them.

The Department of ARPG has taken several initiatives, namely the issue of policy guidelines, setting up internal grievance redress machinery for public and employee grievances in each public office, amendment to rules and computerised monitoring of the effective disposal of grievances. The Department has published a booklet containing the guidelines, which stipulate prompt acknowledgement, effective action on the grievance within prescribed time limits, detailing reasons while sending a reply to the applicant, tracking grievances through computer-compatible numbers, special action for vulnerable groups, announcing and enforcing specific times for meeting people in office, dealing with the public on telephone and facilities for lodging complaints over the counter or on the internet.

Wide publicity has been given to the grievance redress machinery, together with a comprehensive directory containing the names, telephone numbers and locations of all the directors of grievance redress. An officer of the rank of joint secretary is designated as director of grievances in each ministry and department with powers to monitor grievances and to call for papers relating to the disposal of grievances filed by members of the public and employees. The National Informatics Centre has developed and installed uniform software called the public grievance redress and monitoring system in consultation with Department of ARPG for installation in different departments. A citizen can now lodge his or her grievance on the website for grievance redress and can monitor the action taken.

The Department of ARPG has categorised public and employee grievances under distinct categories such as delay, misbehaviour, harassment, corruption, pensioner problems, non-payment of dues etc., on the basis of detailed analysis. The department takes up a certain proportion of grievances on the basis of their gravity and recurrence for intensive monitoring until their resolution. A 'fast track' mechanism was developed to assess the responsiveness of various government agencies, with special reference to departments with a large public interface. These grievances are pursued with regular interventions at the highest level for speedy redress.

In the field of employee grievances, the Department of ARPG has requested all ministries and departments to look into procedures relating to personnel management within their organisation in order to bring about adequate transparency in matters such as time-bound disposal of staff grievances, the machinery available for it and its effectiveness, fixing pay, confirmation, seniority, reservation, availability of recruitment rules, adequate work environment with availability of basic amenities, welfare measures, expeditious settlement of disciplinary cases, effective functioning of staff and departmental levels, empanelment, etc.

Time norms for disposal applications and requests for services or activities which bring the public in contact with the ministry or department have been fixed by government. These time limits are advertised so as to ensure improved public interface and greater accountability. Departments have been instructed to establish an institutional mechanism to take action on grievances reported in newspapers. Systemic deficiencies and centralisation leading to recurring grievances will be taken up for urgent corrective action. The Citizen's Charter will also cover commitments in this regard. Grievance redress will be decentralised to the lowest possible field formations with built-in participatory systems of evaluation. Many ministries have established single window systems at points of public contact wherever possible to facilitate dealing with of applications.

### *Box 5.3* Implementing the Grievance Redress System

**The central government *Manual of Office Procedure* (and departmental manuals of large ministries like Railways) set time limits for dealing with grievances, while the Code of Conduct Rules envisage disciplinary action in case of discourteous behaviour or negligence in grievance disposal. The Annual Confidential Role (ACR) includes a column for employee attitude to grievance redress and interaction with the public. The Department of ARPG undertakes studies to investigate the causes of recurring complaints and departmental procedures and assists departments in reducing systemic causes of complaints. It is pursuing with departments the question of fixing responsibility and preventing evasive replies that frustrate applicants.**

The Department of ARPG is working on a public grievance rating system with World Bank support for departments as part of the movement for the Citizen's Charter and quality government. The rating model will address the receipt and registration of grievances, redress mechanisms, record keeping/reporting and communication relating to grievance redress and management review, system changes, measuring citizen satisfaction, criteria for self-assessment and accountability.

The annual action plan and annual reports of organisations which are placed before Parliament describe the machinery for redress of public and staff grievances and the details of their receipt and disposal.

### *Review Mechanisms*

The Directorate of Public Grievances in the Cabinet Secretariat has functioned since 1988 as an Ombudsman for looking intensively into individual grievances relating to 16 central departments with a large public interface. The Directorate has the authority to call for relevant files from concerned organisations and make suitable considerations for consideration by the department after enquiry. Its recommendations are invariably implemented.

Departments like Insurance and Banking have appointed ombudsmen. Railways have an elaborate and decentralised system for resolving the complaints of the public and employees. Central ministries like Railways, Posts and Telecommunications have set up lok adalats (public courts) to resolve complaints in the presence of consumers.

A standing committee of secretaries and scientific officers under the chairmanship of the Cabinet Secretary reviews the performance of all ministries and departments in public grievance redress and issues directions for improvement. The Department of ARPG interacts periodically with state governments to share experiences on the redress of public grievances. The government is strengthening the legal machinery of countrywide consumer courts for providing expeditious relief to the parties against alleged malpractices by public and private agencies, such as overcharging, poor service quality and breakdown of service. Standing committees of Parliament examine and report on the record of departments in responding to and acting on grievances.

### *Grievance Redress in States*

All state governments have instituted systems for time-bound redress of public grievances with varying degrees of efficiency and responsiveness. Departments in charge of public grievances on the model of central government have been set up in many states. Some of the important institutional arrangements include monitoring by the Chief Minister's Secretariat. The Delhi government has established the Public Grievance Redress Commission. The disposal of grievances is monitored through computerised systems in several states. District officers in a number of north-eastern states and others are required to visit villages collectively under the leadership of the Collector to deal with people's grievances on the spot or initiate time-bound action for complaints needing enquiry.

**Box 5.4 *Praja* and Grievance Redress in Mumbai**

*Praja*, a voluntary agency, is now working actively with the Mumbai Municipal Corporation (MMC) to develop an online grievance redress system. Besides the registration of complaints on the telephone or through a personal visit, citizens can submit complaints online. The system allows the development of a database of the most active portion of the citizenry (i.e. those who complain) that can be mobilised later by e-mail and other means to generate systematic pressure on the MMC to improve services. It also makes it much easier to file complaints and increases the credibility of the process by promising swift action through an independent group. The Mumbai Citizen's Charter was also designed by *Praja* on the basis of consultation with city officials and public feedback on standards. The Charter was simply designed with cartoons and copies were distributed by the daily newspapers. Shortly after, *Praja* conducted and disseminated the first public survey of the BMC performance.

### *Challenges and Reforms*

Despite the existence of these departments and cells, the record of most public agencies in the area of prompt and effective redress of public grievances is uneven across public agencies, especially in the field. Decentralisation of implementation and the association of voluntary agencies and citizen groups in many services are expected to reduce the ills of centralisation. The Conference of Chief Ministers in

1997 endorsed the idea of independent watchdog committees of citizens at district and city level to inspect the functioning of grievance redress mechanisms and report to state grievance redress committees under the Chief Secretary.

For decentralised city wards, the systems introduced in Surat and Mumbai Municipal Corporations deserve study. Under the Andhra Pradesh *Janmabhoomi* programme, officers of various departments at block and village level form a team and visit all the habitations in each block; they conduct village level meetings with the villagers to resolve grievances on the spot and identify community needs that can met through ongoing development programmes. Maharashtra has introduced a *Lokshahi Din*, a pre-announced time in the week, to allow for face-to-face contact between district officers and the public to address problems.

## 5.4 Citizen's Charters

*'A consumer is the most important visitor in our premises. He is not dependent on us, we are dependent on him. He is not an interruption in our work, he is the purpose of it. He is not an outsider to our business, he is part of it. We are not doing him a favour by serving him, he is doing us a favour by giving us an opportunity to do so.'*

Mahatma Gandhi

In the perception of central and state governments, citizen's charters represent the proactive commitment of public agencies to deliver quality services of pre-specified standard, and provide avenues for swift redress in case of deficiency in services. The charters signify the empowerment of user groups through information and consultation. Citizen's charters raise issues of the multiple accountability of government servants: accountability to the executive; to the legislature; to audit; to clients and citizens; and accountability to themselves. Citizen's charters have been formulated in sectors which have a large public interface, such as railways, telecom, post, public distribution systems, hospitals, revenue, electricity and public offices in urban and rural areas. The Charter is operationalised after due orientation of staff and incorporation of public feedback.

The Department of ARPG has issued guidelines for structuring a model charter, as well as a list of do's and don'ts to guide government organisations (see Annex). The charters are expected to incorporate the elements of a vision and mission statement; details of business transacted by the organisation and details of client groups; standards and time limits of services provided to each client group and service delivery mechanism; details of grievance redress mechanism and ways to access it; and clients' expectations. User groups are involved in formulating and evaluating the charters. Computerised information and facilitation counters provide a visible front for the charter for ministries and departments. The effort at the central government level has been guided by a committee chaired by the Secretary (Personnel). The Department of ARPG, as the nodal department, organises workshops to develop trainers and training modules for citizen's charters. Training institutes under various central ministries, the ISTM and state training institutions organise training programmes for skill upgrading and attitudinal orientation of functionaries at policy-making and operational level. The training strategy of the Department of Posts and some nationalised banks has been innovative. Regional seminars were organised to bring national and state level organisations, together with NGOs and stakeholders, to share experiences in the formulation and implementation of charters.

Twenty-four central government ministries, departments and attached organisations have so far issued 93 citizen's charters. A comprehensive website contains details of them. Nodal officers have been appointed by the ministries which have issued the charters. State governments and union territories are reported to have published about 500 citizen's charters so far.

The Department of ARPG is developing a scheme for the award of a 'Charter Mark'. The Mark is a quality standard, which encourages and rewards improvements in public services with reference to the commitments and standards notified in the Charter. Agencies which show a record of exemplary implementation and are providing excellent services, will receive a Charter Mark after independent assessment. The Department is also encouraging experiments to develop benchmarks for quality services across and within departments, based on documentation of good practices. It is envisaged that an external performance audit of all government organisations and offices will take place once in three years, including the evaluation of citizen satisfaction and the implementation of suggestions. Public awareness of the charters is being raised through radio and television programmes and a common logo. Exit polls and public surveys will be organised to evaluate public performance, while structured public private partnerships will build in elements of the Charter as in Bangalore and Delhi cities.

**_Box 5.5_ Citizen's Charters in Nationalised Banks**

**The Department of ARPG has been pursuing the idea of establishing role models of excellence for promoting widespread acceptance of citizen's charters. The banking sector was identified for this purpose because of its advanced thinking in customer service and its use of technology. Three major nationalised banks were brought into the exercise. The issues highlighted were: stakeholder involvement in the formulation of charters; deployment of charters in the banks with the full involvement of staff at all levels; creation of awareness about the charters among customers; study of best practices of private sector banks; and special training for employees at all levels about the concept and implementation of the charters. The status of the charters was evaluated by independent teams and action taken to rectify shortcomings. A widely publicised action plan was drawn up to revise the charter. A training module was developed by the National Institute of Banking Management to encourage more banks to adopt the model.**

### *Citizen's Charters in States*

Following consultation with stakeholders, states have formulated charters for agriculture, animal husbandry and forests, education, electricity and power supply, finance and revenue, food and civil supplies, health, home and police administration, industry, labour and employment, local bodies, social welfare, transport and urban development. In some states user surveys and report cards play an important part in checking progress and revising standards. Hyderabad Metropolitan Water Supply and Sewer Board is remarkable for prescribing time limits and for monitoring its enforcement with NGO inputs. The Government of Gujarat decentralised the issue of citizen's charters to district and sub-district units of various departments. Municipal bodies like Pimpri-Chinchwad have issued service-wide charters. Maharashtra has issued a charter for the state police that allows citizens the right to register a complaint at any police station; the police are obliged to register such complaints immediately and to provide a free copy of the First Information Report (FIR) to the complainant.

### *Model Office*

This concept is linked to the practice of integrated citizen centres referred to earlier. These offices could be part of a state-wide scheme for electronic governance and modernised and responsive services such as the registration of documents and the computerisation of land titles or a network of field offices for revenue departments like sales tax and income tax. The model offices could be part of the effort made by a municipal corporation or development authority to provide improved services across the city and at decentralised levels. The services, again, could be a mix of free or fee-based service, regulation and revenue mobilisation. There could be a network of model offices (linked by LAN or WAN) in a department, that are scattered across the state, as in the case of registration and transport departments; or a network of centres under a municipal government; or a pilot centre under a department. The model offices could provide a single service such as registration or transport for a functional target group, or the office could provide a number of varied services falling under the jurisdiction of the head of office as in the case of revenue officers and municipal commissioner. Finally, the model office could be the location for integrated services to citizens, as described earlier. The district office can also be the hub of participatory district planning as in Kerala or of district government as in Madhya Pradesh.

### *Challenges*

Recent evaluations and feedback have revealed the risks of publishing empty promises in glossily published citizen's charters without positive steps to match the performance to the promises and the rhetoric. Besides client consultation, departments have realised the value of involving and consulting employees at all stages to address their misgivings and gain their support. The quality of implementation of charters is seen as more important than the number of charters issued by government. Hence, attention is being paid to the re-engineering of processes, enforcement of credibly determined time limits, employee ownership and user involvement. Progressive states and central ministries are assessing progress in enforcing standards and in promoting increased access by citizens to information and decisions of departments through independent agencies, user surveys and exit polls. The exercise of the Department of ARPG with the banks shows the way to operationalise the charters.

A further lesson from experience is that, instead of trying to reform all the processes at once with the risk of encountering huge resistance, it might be advisable to break down the changes into small components and tackle them one at a time. It is far more important to consolidate present experience with implementation and to establish credibility among citizens about a few key departments and local authorities with large user interfaces, than to concentrate on the statistics about published charters.

## 5.5 TQM and Improving Quality of Service

Total Quality Management is no longer restricted to manufacturing operations in India, but is expected to permeate all sectors with a customer interface. Quality in government is visualised from the perspectives of information, service delivery, accountability and efficiency. Citizen focus and teamwork require departments to move away from hierarchical and rigid adherence to rules and procedures. Quality improvement is a continuous process and has the potential to integrate activities under a citizen's charter and information technology. The Defence Accounts Department issued a statement of quality policy with a commitment to provide efficient, correct and prompt accounting, payment and financial services, leading to customer satisfaction, and to render audit services to ensure public accountability. Most of its offices have received the ISO 9000 certificate. After identifying the problems faced by customers such as army personnel and by employees, the department formulated counter-measures based on the reports of task forces. The Controller of Defence Accounts implemented a single window system of grievance redress to the vastly increased satisfaction of army personnel in far-flung areas. A number of improvements in procedures and record management were introduced.

A number of departments like ARPG and the Department of Parliamentary Affairs are aiming to apply for the IS 9000 standard in quality performance. Andhra Pradesh has devised a system of performance indicators related to quantitative and quality measures and this is supplemented by external measures of public satisfaction (called *spandana*) on the basis of media reports and independent surveys of public opinion on macro and micro aspects of performance.

**_Box 5.6_ Implementing TQM**

**The implementation of TQM in the department of ARPG has brought together managers and support staff in the framework of capacity building, incentives for model behaviour and reforms in working procedures. A voluntary scheme of awards for model behaviour was notified with the rating based on observance of three factors (clearing, categorising and cleaning), generation of KAIZEN (continuous improvement) and adherence to discipline. Existing processes for dealing with files and correspondence and for dispatch of letters were streamlined.**

**The Department of ARPG has made an arrangement in collaboration with the Quality Division of the Confederation of Indian Industries (CII) to introduce TQM practices in the centre and states and to evaluate current initiatives in organisations like the Department of ARPG, Delhi Sales Tax Department and the Department of Defence Accounts. An excellent publication, _Quality Management in Government_, has emerged out of this evaluation.**

The Ministry of PPGP is implementing a project for introducing TQM in training institutions. This is co-ordinated by LBSNAA. Annual awards are given to central and state training institutions. The objectives are to raise awareness of quality and performance standards in the management of training within government; develop criteria for national standards for training institutes, trainers, consultants through a lead institution in partnership with four or five state level institutes; and apply TQM methodology and techniques to the functioning of government training institutes.

## *Annex*

## Do's and Don't for Implementing Citizen's Charters

| | Do's | Don'ts |
|---|---|---|
| 1 | Make haste, slowly | Don't merely make haste |
| 2 | List areas of interface | Don't be unrealistic |
| 3 | Phase out areas for introduction of small steps | Don't take on more than you can commit to |
| 4 | Involve customers and staff in implementing it | Don't involve only senior officers in the formulation and implementation |
| 5 | Prepare a Master Plan for formulation and implementation | Don't rush into an overall package for the whole ministry/ department/ organisation |
| 6 | Win consumer confidence with small, highly visible measures | Don't promise more than you can deliver |
| 7 | Remember, a Citizen's Charter is a process, constantly evolving | Don't look upon it as a one-time exercise with a final outcome |
| 8 | Inform the customer of the proposed commitments | Don't inform the customer unless you are sure of delivering the service |
| 9 | Use simple language | Don't use difficult language or jargon |
| 10 | Train your staff | Don't leave yourself out |
| 11 | Delegate power | Don't centralise |
| 12 | Set up systems for feedback and independent scrutiny | Don't continue blindly without periodic reassessment of performance |

# 6 Reaching Out to People and Stakeholders

## 6.1 Documentation and Dissemination of Good Practices and Policies

***Government Initiatives***

Over the years, many initiatives in good governance have been taken by central and state governments, as well as by individual agencies and employees. However, the documentation of best practice is often confined to newspaper reports and official briefs. This is largely due to the fact that the people involved in the process have little time or patience to document it. In the absence of professional documentation, it is neither possible to evaluate the initiative or to replicate a worthy model.

The Department of ARPG has brought out documentation about best practice in printed and video formats to compile information and experiences on various initiatives and projects. This can also be used as training material. The Department has issued guidelines to central ministries and states for undertaking similar documentation and offers financial support, as in the case of the experiment of *Bhagidari* (partnership) in Delhi. The Department publishes a monthly newsletter, *Civil Service News*, and a quarterly journal, *Management in Government*. It also publishes case studies on administration in different organisations for the benefit of central ministries, training institutions and states.

Between March 2000 and September 2001, the Department organised a series of 20 lectures on the subject 'Ideas that have worked'. The lectures were delivered by eminent personalities who have made a mark in the public or private sector by achieving outstanding results, setting up remarkable institutions or turning around institutions. The lectures were converted into documentary films and broadcast on television.

The Department of ARPG has developed a series of documentary films demonstrating best practice in e-governance entitled *Information Technology in the Service of Citizen*. The first eight films will cover outstanding programmes in various states, such as e-Seva and *Bhoomi*. The films will be produced by the Prasar Bharati (national organisation for visual media) and then telecast on national and regional television. Similar efforts are being made by other central ministries like the Ministries of Health and Human Resources Development.

LBSNAA and a number of state training institutions document good practices and use them as case studies for training and policy-level discussions. The Centre for Good Governance (CGG) in Andhra Pradesh is creating a repertoire of case studies and evaluations for assisting sector departments.

**_Box 6.1_ Non-governmental Initiatives for Disseminating Best Practices**

**Civil society and professionals outside government recognise that it was not sufficient to disseminate best practices or train officials. It is vital to assist interested agencies or individuals in the adaptive implementation of good practices. An instance of mediation by peer groups is the establishment of the City Managers Association by mayors, city managers and urban professionals in Ahmedabad (Gujarat). The Association undertakes the documentation and dissemination of best practices after validation in seminars of elected representatives and city officials. The Association then encourages the transfer of replicable good practices based on peer support and training. It has strengthened learning networks of city managers in a number of states and is working together with national and state governments in areas like waste management, property taxation, slum improvement, contracting for services, municipal accounting and similar areas.**

**Building centres, which are funded by a national and financial organisation, but operated by an independent society or NGO, represent another instance of innovative ways to disseminate appropriate and low-cost technology and undertake training of local artisans.**

## 6.2 Establishing Partnerships with Stakeholders and User Groups

One of the dimensions of a proactive government is the emergence of public-private partnerships and support for the initiatives of the poor, city level planning, economic enterprises and transport. Partnerships broaden the range and deepen the base of participation at local and neighbourhood level. Partnerships in India are horizontal and vertical, government-led and citizen-driven, depending on who takes the lead.

Partnerships with voluntary agencies, financial institutions and stakeholders are structured into many centrally sponsored programmes and externally aided projects for social services, poverty reduction and infrastructure. There are many city level partnerships of municipal council and citizen groups for shelter upgrading, slum improvement, health care and waste management, such as EXNORA in Chennai. The private sector is increasingly a part of such partnerships where it can provide both managerial skills and in-fill finance. Professional managers form associations to validate and spread innovations as in the case of the City Managers Association, the All India Mayors Council and the All India Management Association.

Some local partnerships have expanded into national movements with government support as in the case of the National Women's Fund for supporting women's savings groups, slum dweller and pavement collectives and street children. Voluntary agencies can help to build the knowledge and capacity of poor families for livelihood support and service provision. In other cities, peer networks have seeded partnerships as in the case of pavement women from Mumbai or the collective of women elected representatives in Karnataka.

Partnerships of government with business also take shape in ways other than joint sector investments and contracting for services. Economic ministries like the Ministries of Commerce and Industry have formed export promotion councils and industrial promotion committees with the active membership of concerned industries. Government representatives participate in annual deliberations of industry federations at national and regional level and the consensus leads to reforms in laws, policies and procedures. The Prime Minister has constituted an advisory council of experts and task forces in different sectors composed of leading industrialists to advise him and the economic ministers on policy directions. In cities like Indore, the corporate sector is helping low-income communities to map out competitive strategies for their businesses, while it is partnering local bodies in cities like Ahmedabad in upgrading slums. Government encourages such ventures through tax breaks and policy guidelines.

### *State and Local Initiatives*

Partnerships are much more productive at the decentralised level because they affect services of critical importance to citizens. People's initiatives express themselves in several ways – citizens' groups, neighbourhood organisations, associations to safeguard community interests and culture, pressure groups, voluntary organisations to protect the rights of the people in general and the vulnerable and marginal groups in particular, trade unions and co-operatives. The 73rd and 74th amendments on decentralisation have strengthened the capacity of local self-government to interact with civil society.

**_Box 6.2_ Local Partnerships**

**The Mumbai Urban Transport Project has led to a unique partnership of central and state agencies with slum dwellers association and SPARC, a voluntary agency, for participatory relocation of slums located on rail tracks. A similar partnership on slum sanitation in Mumbai and Pune, and programmes of beneficiary-driven rural water supply, have raised the credibility of government programmes with poor and marginal citizen groups.**

**The Ahmedabad Municipal Corporation took the initiative in organising a partnership of the local body, voluntary agencies and business groups to facilitate the efforts of slum dwellers to upgrade services and shelter through sharing costs and management of different components. Bangalore Action Task Force is a model for the partnership of business, public agencies, civil society groups and academic experts for catalyzing various initiatives in Bangalore. Similar models can be found in Mumbai, Baroda and Ahmedabad.**

## 6.3 Involving Employees

An innovative measure designed by the Department of ARPG to achieve higher productivity in public organisations was the introduction of Work Improvement Teams (WITs) in a few sequential steps. A small group of members of a unit would identify an operational problem and remit it to a steering committee in the ministry or public enterprise for consideration. The scheme also provided for appropriate training for the team leaders in various institutions. The scheme was introduced in selected organisations which have a large interface with the public.

### *National Award Scheme*

An award scheme is being implemented by the Department from 1998–99 for central government employees as well as members of the public to come up with innovative and workable suggestions for improving the quality of public services and making it more customer-friendly. This scheme has been revamped as 'National Award Scheme 2001' and widely publicised. Suggestions received from employees as well as members of the public are being scrutinised by the respective departmental evaluation committees of ministries and departments, and their recommendations are further considered by an apex committee under the chairmanship of the Secretary (Personnel). Suggestions which can lead to financial savings through reduction of manpower and material or which can enhance efficiency and productivity through procedural improvements and reduced paper work, time taken or public satisfaction in government offices will be considered for an award. Awards will also be given to outstanding central government operational staff for their meritorious services under the scheme.

### *Adopting New Work Habits*

Officers and staff have been addressed to promote a new work culture by giving more importance to results rather than procedures, looking at requests from the members of the public from the users' point of view and not solely from the point of view of what might be administratively convenient, and showing more sensitivity to the needs and aspirations of the people.

# 7 Decentralisation and People's Participation

## 7.1 Co-operative Federalism

The Indian Constitution has a federal character with a distinct unitary bias. This was a conscious decision to ensure the unity and integrity of a heterogeneous country with multiple languages, religions and ethnic groups. The Constitution provides for multi-level governance, with both the central and state governments having their own executive, legislature and judiciary and exercising powers according to a division and lists mandated in the Constitution. At the same time, most areas of governance of critical importance for citizens are at the state and local level: public order, justice, rule of law, school education, health care, most of the road network, electrical power, agriculture, rural development, urban planning and local government. The seven union territories enjoy less authority and financial powers and are inferior in status to the state governments.

The central government's dominance is evident in the division of resources, its authority to issue directions to state governments in financial and security matters, powers to impose emergency in states under stipulated circumstances and the power of Parliament to create new states or enact legislation in areas earmarked for states. The institutions of the All India Services and Comptroller and Auditor General are a means to integrated administration and audit. The national planning process and control over investments, control over industrial licensing and regulation, the power to channel external aid and funding under centrally sponsored schemes, have all combined to increase the financial dependence of states on the central government.

Various factors have made the quality of states' own economic and social management and public administration a more important determinant of growth and pro-poor performance: the political changes in the 1990s, variations in levels of growth and human development indices and huge fiscal deficits in the states. Both the central government and donor agencies like the World Bank have recognised that it is critical to accelerate state reforms by local partnerships and structural adjustment loans and Memoranda of Understanding between state governments and the Central Finance Ministry. There has been a serious effort to transfer central schemes to the states and to ensure greater predictability in the devolution of central revenues to the states on the basis of the awards of federal finance commissions. However, a matter of serious concern is the increasing disparity in economic growth and human development indicators among different states, arising partly from varying political commitment to good governance and administrative capacity.

The emergence of different political parties in control of state governments and growing impatience with various forms of central control have led to the advocacy of co-operative federalism resting on a spirit of mutual trust and expeditious resolution of disputes based on broader national concerns. Central and state governments have taken a number of decisions following the report of the Sarkaria Commission on Centre-State Relations.

There is more political space for states to mark out their own course, especially as governments tend to be more stable in many states. The Constitution has been amended to ensure that a fixed proportion of the divisible pool of taxes is transferred to the states. The enabling environment provided by states has become an important determinant of investment flows due to trends in economic liberalisation and there is greater freedom and diversity for state governments in various matters of economic and social policy.

The central government will of course need to continue to play the role of co-ordinator and mediator in inter-state matters, while ensuring that the more backward states are not left behind in economic development and the fight against poverty. While having to negotiate with states on federal issues, the central government is also navigating the economy through the dynamic forces of free trade in the SAARC (South Asian Association for Regional Co-operation) region, globalisation and international trade. In times of heightened concern for security, central government plays a critical role in external defence and internal security.

**Box 7.1 Co-operative Federalism and the Inter State Council**

**Central to the idea of co-operative federalism is negotiation and co-operation. This is facilitated by the constitutional mechanism of the Inter State Council where matters of mutual interest can be discussed and decided by central and state governments, often through subject committees. The National Commission to Review the Working of the Constitution has endorsed the importance of the Council. Recent activities include the formation of committees under the Prime Minister/ Deputy Prime Minister to decide on the future directions of good governance, barriers to trade across and within states, setting up an investor-friendly climate and e-governance. The sub-committee on governance will monitor the action plan for good governance and conceptualise strategies to reform the revenue administration, encourage public-private partnerships and implement judicial and urban sector reforms. It will also suggest a framework for linking the flow of funds and central assistance to the implementation of mutually agreed reforms of governance.**

The Planning Commission has undertaken a detailed exercise to identify the centrally sponsored schemes to be transferred to the states and to lay down the principles for the direct involvement of central ministries in areas reserved to them. Central planning is seen as a necessary complement to a decentralised, flexible and co-operative mode of development planning and and as a means of promoting equity between poor and affluent classes, rural and urban areas, and backward and prosperous states.

The National Development Council provides a forum for deciding the contours of economic planning, the size of public investment and the formula for distributing plan assistance with due regard for more liberal terms for backward states. The Council also discusses issues relating to food, agriculture, power, irrigation, centrally sponsored schemes and land reform. The other fora include the conferences of state governors and chief secretaries, zonal conferences of chief ministers and the National Water Resources Council.

A development in the virtuous cycle is the increasing competition among states to attract domestic and foreign investment and innovate in various areas of administration and technology. One of the reasons is the contagion effect as innovations in one state become candidates for adoption in other states. Media and business associations are rating the states in terms of good governance and investor-friendly regimes and political leaders are sensitive to such assessment. Central government intervenes to prevent a vicious cycle of subsidies and populist concessions in states and to ensure equitable exploitation of rivers and natural resources.

Federalism has been taken to a decentralised level following the 73rd and 74th constitutional amendments, which have elevated the status of elected local bodies and set up district planning committees to sustain people's participation. The realisation of the goals of decentralisation requires the states to display to local bodies the same spirit of accommodation that the states expect the central government to show towards them in matters of devolution of resources and powers.

## 7.2 Democratic Decentralisation in Rural and Urban Areas

It is useful to note that local self-government is part of Indian heritage over many centuries, and that this was noted in Article 40 of the Indian Constitution. Local government falls under the control of state governments, based on laws and regulations affecting their structure, functions, finances, personnel and state control. However, the 1992 constitutional amendments have elevated the *Panchayati Raj* Institutions and the Urban Local Bodies or municipalities (ULBs) to the level of a third tier of government, with assigned functions and commensurate resources. The Constitution provides for the establishment of district planning committees, composed of elected representatives, to prepare social and economic plans based on consultation.

The PRIs consist of tiers at the level of districts, blocks and villages, while the ULBs consist of municipal corporations and councils. The Constitution also provides for the reservation of one-third of seats in these bodies to women and scheduled castes and tribes. As with the Federal Commission, state finance commissions recommend the pattern of tax assignment and sharing and devolution of grants by state governments to urban and rural local bodies.

There are 532 district panchayats and 5,912 block/mandal panchayats, of which more than 175 districts have women presidents and 1,970 blocks have women presidents. There are 231,630 village panchayats, 95 city municipal corporations and 3,481 municipalities with varying powers and functions according to particular state laws.

In the perception of the government, the village panchayat is as autonomous as the municipality in urban areas, and the *Gram sabhas* should be enabled to play a leading role in the identification of local needs, identification of beneficiaries of schemes, mobilisation of local resources and preparation of plans, and the monitoring of local projects.

All the states have enacted amendments to existing laws to ensure compliance with the Constitution and have also held elections to the appropriate bodies. Central government has promulgated the Panchayats (Election to Scheduled Areas) Act to endow panchayats in scheduled tribal areas with greater powers and control over resources.

State governments have also acted on the reports of state finance commissions and many have assigned a definite share of state revenues to local bodies. Performance norms have been prescribed in some states for different urban services. Kerala and Madhya Pradesh have created a separate category of district budget to provide a transparent allocation of funds. Karnataka and other states have increased funding to panchayats which is not tied to specific schemes along with increased local tax sources. The Federal Finance Commission has also awarded funds to be channelled automatically to local bodies by the states.

In order to make panchayats and municipalities full-fledged institutions of local self-government, Kerala state has transferred to them important public service institutions such as Krishi Bhavans, veterinary hospitals, primary health centres and government dispensaries, primary and high schools, pre-school and nutrition centres, village and district roads, small-scale industries and co-operative institutions. The elected representatives of the panchayats and municipalities are responsible for managing these institutions and for supervising and controlling their staff from the doctor to the healthworker and from the agriculture officer to the farm labourer. This has enhanced the local accountability of important government delivery systems and has created an enthusiastic response to sorting out the problems of the common man. This is accompanied by a widespread involvement of voluntary agencies.

In a remarkable example of bottom-up planning, people's campaigns have been organised with the support of voluntary resource persons to identify the development needs of the people, indicate their priorities and suggest solutions. In West Bengal state, path-breaking efforts have been made to institutionalise the system of district and block planning committees. Panchayats have been given responsibility for distribution of vested lands, and construction of minor irrigation facilities, roads and other infrastructure.

### Challenges and Prospects

Despite the political rhetoric on decentralisation, the progress in complete devolution is uneven across the states in terms of effective functional and financial autonomy and the organisational effectiveness of the local bodies. In a number of states, there is a built-in resistance in the state political and administrative leadership to the dilution of centralised control over local schemes and to the transfer of schemes, staff and funds to the PRIs and ULBs. Not all states have transferred functions to the local bodies as envisaged under the Constitution.

The lingering concerns and constraints pointed out by the Planning Commission and other observers in respect of the PRIs include: the need for clarity in the distribution of functions between the three tiers; the clarification of the role of deconcentrated field units of state government and the Collector in the districts; confusion over the co-location of the village panchayat with user-managed activities; inadequate capacity of PRI functionaries; total dependence on government funds; and the prudent use of funds.

Many states have empowered the PRIs to exercise control over education, health care and a number of development activities, which were previously under the control of state departments. The role of the *Gram sabha* has been increasingly stressed, with some states setting up ward or *Vasathi sabhas* in all the gram panchayat members' constituencies to give more opportunities to local people to participate in panchayat activities and thereby ensure transparency and accountability in governance. Emphasis has been placed on active participation in decision making by weaker sections, to enhance their role, status and leadership in PRIs. Block resource centres have been set up with the help of NGOs to provide information on development schemes and procedures to the elected representatives and the people.

The concept of public hearing of local officials and political leaders has gained ground following the striking experience of the citizen movement of MKSS (struggle of farmers and labour) in Rajasthan.

The personnel in rural local government have been generally composed of officers on deputation from state departments. In the case of municipalities, there are varying practices in states, with some states permitting municipal corporations to recruit and manage their cadres and other states setting up state level municipal cadres. Some states have transferred the staff along with the functions entrusted to the PRIs and have set up a separate development service for rural local bodies. States are giving increasing control to village panchayats over their staff.

### *Box 7.2* Responding to Pressures for Local Empowerment

**The states are responding to growing pressures from the grassroots for empowerment and the advocacy of central government. A number of states have successfully addressed these concerns through legal amendments, widespread training programmes, constitution of district planning committees under the chairmanship of the chairperson of the Zilla Parishad (district tier of PRI), converting user bodies into committees of the village panchayat, asserting the supremacy of the council of the village population (*Gram sabha*) and social audit of PRI working. State and regional associations of women elected representatives have been pushing vigorously for greater devolution of untied funds and mandates to the panchayats. Kerala launched an innovative people's campaign for development by enabling the local population to prepare development plans within a given resource envelope and then consolidating these plans to formulate the district plan and budget.**

Thanks to central financial leverage and advocacy, and the demonstration of strong political support for decentralisation in a number of states, the PRIs and ULBs are becoming established as organs of local self-government. During the tenth Five-year Plan, there will be an increasing flow of resources to the local bodies under various development schemes. The selection of beneficiaries for these schemes would be done by the *Gram sabha*. The Ministry of Rural Development has issued detailed instructions for a social audit of all development works at the village level.

### *Urban Local Bodies*

The problems of the urban local bodies are similar but more acute than those of the PRIs, since urbanisation and municipalisation have not proceeded in parallel. Progress is again uneven across states, depending on the tradition of vibrant local government, with Maharashtra, Gujarat, Kerala and West Bengal taking the lead. The proliferation of state parastatal agencies for different areas of urban infrastructure has tended to undermine the legitimate role of elected local bodies. There has been a delay in some states in setting up ward committees with citizen representatives.

Citizen movements and the strident advocacy of elected municipal representatives has led to greater willingness of states to vest stronger executive authority in mayors and mayor-in-council, channel additional development funds through municipalities, enable the reform of property tax and user charges and organise training programmes for urban functionaries. Incentives for state level reform are available through funding from central government and financial institutions, linked to reforms in municipal regulations, management and finances, and enabling pooled financing facility for a number of small municipalities. Karnataka has entered into a Memorandum of Understanding with Bangalore and other large city corporations to ensure a performance-based system of resource transfer and local effort.

## 7.3 User Management of Services

### *Approach and Examples*

The poverty reduction strategies of government and the management of natural resources since the 1970s have emphasised the critical role of community participation and the involvement of user agencies. With central encouragement, many states have in the past few years enthusiastically supported the strategy of community involvement by forming user group committees for the implementation of their developmental plans and programmes and the management of natural resources. This approach has paid rich dividends, as demonstrated by the success of programmes like Joint Forest Management (JFM), Participatory Irrigation Management (PIM), the *Swajal* rural water supply project and the watershed mission. This is paralleled by support to co-operatives in agriculture, dairy and other economic sectors.

In the field of livelihood support, government is shifting from direct individual assistance to encouragement of the formation of self-help groups (SHGs), predominantly composed of women. At government instance or on their own, NGOs and local bodies are building up the capabilities of SHGs for the management of funds and activities and providing information on activity clusters, marketing and finance.

**_Box 7.3_ Approaches to User Management of Services**

**Successful approaches to user management in watershed, forestry and irrigation have often graduated into strategies for community empowerment, and partnerships are taken a step forward through support for user management of health and education services. Governments at central and state level provide encouragement for the formation of village committees and urban neighbourhood groups, with links to wider government networks, for the management of individual activities like primary schools, watershed, irrigation channels, shelter upgrading, slum relocation, family welfare, primary health care and urban waste collection. They offer programme support through local volunteers, and assistance from NGOs for training and accessing organised institutions. The schemes for urban and rural development extend support for the formation of development groups of women and youth. Government policy of working towards universal literacy emphasises local ownership and participation through village committees of parents and the panchayat. Some states have entrusted the management of hospitals to patient welfare societies and local advisory committees oversee the work of primary health centres.**

Andhra Pradesh has one of the most vibrant self-help group movements in India, with about 100,000 such registered groups that have mobilised total savings of over Rs. 2 billion. The SHGs (usually composed of women) are able to widen their sphere of operations though flexible support provided by a district poverty initiative project, which is operated by a poverty eradication commission. Similar initiatives are found in other states. Women-based SHGs have expanded into literacy projects and projects that fight alcoholism and work on health and nutrition.

A number of states, for example Andhra Pradesh, Karnataka, Bihar,

Goa, Gujarat, Orissa and Uttar Pradesh, have entrusted the operation and management of water resources at distributary and canal levels to water user association of farmers. These arrangements have led to tremendous improvements in the spread, efficiency and equity of water use, the maintenance of canals and the integration of water use with farm practices. A systematic analysis of the reasons for the success, as well as the challenges faced by the effort, is providing pointers to how co-operation between community members can be induced with the right incentives – lessons that may be applicable to similar models for managing a range of services, including those in health, education and sanitation,

In urban areas, neighbourhood groups of poor families are federated at the city level and form links with other groups of women and slum dwellers. The urban basic services programme is backstopped by community workers attached to the municipal council. City development plans help to make assistance from various government sources and financial institutions congruent with the priorities of the local population, as seen in projects in the cities of Mallapuram, Hyderabad, Vishakapatnam, Indore and Pune. Urban resident associations handle a number of maintenance functions such as the collection of service charges, maintenance of community parks and amenities, streetlights, meter reading and overseeing the quality of road construction.

To cope with concerns about tensions between user groups and elected local bodies, Andhra Pradesh has set up a local collective of *janmabhoomi* and user groups under the chairmanship of the Sarpanch (head of the panchayat). Other states have set up committees under the panchayat with the approval of the *Gram sabha* to deal with the problem of co-location of user committees under different schemes. Institutional solutions have been devised such as the district rural/urban development agency to build convergence among programmes run by different departments and voluntary agencies, bearing on a beneficiary target group like poor women, poor people living in slums, children in difficult circumstances, the pre-school programme or farmers in a watershed area.

## 7.4 Citizen Movements and Enforcing Accountability

Where large and unresponsive public agencies have a monopoly over many services, mechanisms for improved accountability are more important than exit. Report card, user surveys, public hearing, citizen's charter and budget analysis offer a way of supplementing the traditional accountability and oversight mechanisms in ways that place a premium on transparency, participation and support from civil society.

### *Box 7.4* Report Card and Citizen Services

An exercise was initiated by the Public Affairs Centre (PAC) in Bangalore city in 1993 to collect feedback from users on the quality, efficiency and adequacy of the various services. The perceptions in the scientific Gallup Poll exercise were aggregated to create a 'report card' that rated the performance of all major service providers in the city. The findings presented a quantitative measure of satisfaction and perceived levels of corruption. Following coverage in the media, the findings not only mobilised citizen and government support for reform, but also prompted the rated agencies themselves to respond positively to civic calls for improvement in services. Report cards became a useful medium through which citizens could credibly and collectively 'signal' to agencies about their performance and mount pressure for change.

The exercise has been replicated in other Indian cities to assess the response of different types of users and sectors such as health, the public distribution system and industrial regulation, e-governance and freedom of information. Comparative assessments of cities and states were also undertaken. PAC undertook, from the citizens' perspective, the first comprehensive assessment across Indian states of the state of public services such as primary education, health care, drinking water, public transport and public distribution, which impact on the welfare of the majority of the population. More importantly, PAC has been able to support ventures by NGOs and research agencies in other Indian cities to assess public services and conditions in slums. The versatility of the tool is demonstrated by the use of the report card in countries like Bangladesh and Ukraine.

#### *Partnership-based Campaigns*

Public agencies at local, state and central level have responded positively once citizen networks started operating on equal terms on the basis of knowledge and research. This was demonstrated by the experience of many citizen networks in Bangalore such as CIVIC and the Committee of Bangalore Residents Associations (COBRA) and the multi-stakeholder forum called the Bangalore Agenda Task Force. Similar networks of residents' associations formed to press areas of citizen concern emerged in other cities such as Chennai (waste management), Mumbai (public distribution system) and Kolkata (conservation) to which the public agencies responded. Baroda Citizens' Council continues to function as an innovative city level group of business, NGOs and municipal representatives which supports NGO- and citizen-led actions for improved services and livelihood. Similar networks have emerged in Mumbai and other cities. Delhi presents an excellent example of *Bhagidari* or partnership between the Delhi government at the neighbourhood and city level to discuss and respond sensitively to various issues of immediate concern to citizens.

**_Box 7.5_ Public Reporting of Performance of Local Agencies**

**The PROOF (Public Reporting of Operations of Finance) campaign in Karnataka, supported by the Chief Minister, demonstrates how urban agencies can build confidence among citizens with quarterly statements from PROOF giving full and accurate performance information to the city's various stakeholders. These reviews are also catalysts in a larger process of bringing government and public closer together. In practical terms, each review acts as a benchmark and provides a basis for developing, reshaping and accelerating other mechanisms of analysis and participation. Performance indicators, qualitative and quantitative, have been developed for education and health in the first phase.**

**The Bangalore Action Task Force (BATF) has been working as a catalyst since 2000 with full government partnership and subsumes PROOF. While the stakeholders set the targeted goals based on citizen feedback, BATF helps them to implement them whenever needed. BATF has also taken up projects on its own initiative to build credibility with the stakeholders, and showcase best practices. It has, directly or through private trusts, seed-funded many innovative projects such as 'Nirmala (spotless) Bangalore', 'Swachcha (clean) Bangalore' and road improvement, and has committed about Rs. 180 million from donations.**

### *Citizen Movements*

Citizen movements in different parts of the country are coming together to strengthen advocacy on issues of national importance such as freedom of information, reforms in electoral law, devolution of powers to elected local bodies and curbing corruption. The struggle of the MKSS in Rajasthan displayed the vital link between the right to information and survival for poor farmers and workers. The leading civil society agencies, supported by experts, lent support to a major reform of the election law to oblige candidates in different elections to disclose to the returning officer details of their educational qualifications, assets and liabilities, and criminal record. With efforts by civil society to give wide publicity to these details, there are brighter prospects for the nomination of candidates with a clean record. Following this, the constitutional amendment to penalise defections has been passed while the Bill on campaign finance reform is on the anvil. The citizen movement on budget analysis was described above.

Citizen pressure and enforcing accountability sometimes takes the form of a public interest petition before the High Court or the Supreme Court on executive acts of omission and commission and issues of vital concern such as pollution control, rehabilitation of population affected by projects, building regulations, corruption in high life, the plight of under-trial prisoners and waste of public funds. Government has often co-operated with the judiciary in agreeing to legal and institutional reforms in areas like the investigation of corrupt activities, enforcement of the use of non-polluting auto fuel, amendment to building laws, dispute resolution and prevention of harassment of women employees.

### *Consulting the People*

Structural adjustment programmes and fiscal corrective measures have to be conveyed in meaningful terms to diverse sections of society, including the poor and marginal groups, such as the re-ordering of expenditure to improve services and allocations for non-salary components of education and health. State governments have made transparent declaration of the nature and causes of fiscal crisis in White Papers laid before the legislature and media in an instance of proactive accountability. Andhra Pradesh started the practice of pre-budget consultation on the budget document. There is a wealth of information on government policies, departmental activities and circulars on the portals hosted by central ministries, and state and local governments.

### *The Role of Non-governmental Organisations*

The role of NGOs has been recognised in the strategy for planned development and sector policies. It is reported that there are over 1,000,000 NGOs at national and local levels with an agenda of development, advocacy, philanthropy and research. Government has been careful to install a transparent regulatory system to assure the public about the development credentials of voluntary agencies. The process of citizen consultation on development issues is sometimes mediated by civil society as in the case of independent surveys of public services undertaken by NGOs in Karnataka and Orissa, or the survey of problems of business and industry by federations of industry and commerce.

> ***Box 7.6* NGOs and Development**
>
> **The ministries in charge of health and other social sector ministries formulate national policies on the basis of wide consultation and have structured partnerships with voluntary agencies and experts. NGOs are involved by central and state departments in supporting citizen initiatives, building the capacity of self-help groups, training and the direct delivery of services. The Ministry of Rural Development has set up an agency called CAPART for the structured involvement of NGOs in rural development and watershed development programmes. Financial institutions help to mainstream and enlarge NGO initiatives for community-based savings and credit systems. A nodal cell in the Planning Commission deals with cross-sector problems of NGOs relating to registration, regulation and access to funds from Indian and international sources. Specialised institutes of management and national level NGOs provide training and research support to professionals in NGOs.**

In Bihar and other states, there are several prominent examples of successful NGO and NGO-partnered activities such as primary and secondary education, AIDS awareness and prevention programmes, the polio eradication programme, family planning services, the anti-leprosy campaign, the dairy sector and women's self-help groups.

Central government has been responsive to campaigns and representations, focusing on basic principles of governance. These include the right to information, the right to shelter for the homeless, rehabilitation of population displaced by projects, community oversight of development works and expenditure, action against delinquent political and official functionaries, representation of citizens in ward committees and the protection of people from the adverse environmental consequences of industrial and extractive activities.

Consumer associations in general or groups representing specific services have been active for a long time in advocating quality standards, tariff regulation, display of prices and product features, and the rights of consumers against manufacturers and service providers. A separate ministry in charge of consumer affairs has been set up in central government to interact continuously with recognised national and state consumer bodies and to provide financial assistance for product testing, surveys and research. A progressive law on redress of consumer grievances has been the enacted, leading to the establishment of consumer courts at state and district level.

# 8 Electronic Governance

## 8.1 Organising for E-governance

### *Central Government Initiatives*

E-governance harnesses information and communication technologies (ICT) such as the internet, the worldwide web and mobile phones to deliver information to citizens and business, improve decision-making and functioning of government and enhance efficiency of service delivery and joined-up government. The objective of electronic governance, in government's view, goes far beyond mere computerisation of stand-alone back-office operations. It is not about hardware and software but marks a fundamental change in the way government operates and interacts with citizens.

A sub-committee of the Inter State Council is looking into all issues affecting e-governance at the central and state level. At the central level, a High Powered Committee (HPC) for improving administrative efficiency by using IT in Government has been set up under the chairmanship of the Cabinet Secretary. This committee has prepared an action plan with over 20 modules. The responsibility for e-governance is shared by the Department of Information Technology (DIT) and the Department of ARPG. DIT is responsible for policy matters relating to IT as a whole.

The operative elements of e-governance include:

- The creation of the necessary legal and administrative framework through the enactment of the Information Technology (IT) Act, 2000 and necessary amendment of all central laws and manuals to enable electronic transactions;

- A 12-Point Minimum Agenda for promotion of e-governance in the functioning of ministries and departments, encompassing areas such as computer availability, Local Area Network, training and capacity building in IT, use of e-mail and e-enabling official processes such as grievance redress, setting up websites, electronic publication of information, making available forms on the website, enabling submission of forms online and e-delivery of citizen services;
- Identification of agencies and areas of large interface with citizens and business for IT applications, such as public grievances, police and the issue of certificates and permits;
- Encouraging ministries and agencies to re-engineer procedures and to devote at least 2 per cent of budget provision to computerisation;
- Supporting the establishment of dedicated departments for IT in state governments and extending help through the National Informatics Centre and centrally sponsored programmes, sharing of best practices, channelling international assistance, etc.;
- Establishment of the Centre for Electronic Governance and National Institute of Smart Governance (with private partnership) for showcasing tools and applications, replication of success stories and re-engineering of processes;
- Designation of IT managers in departments to spearhead the application of IT and build computer literacy at all levels;
- Setting up in the Department of ARPG a digital repository and resource centre to provide reference materials, user manuals, standards, templates, common solutions and tools for business process re-engineering, use of IT and capacity building;

Besides the projects listed in Box 8.1, initiatives for computerisation of operations have been taken by the Election Commission, Postal Department, Employee Provident Fund Organisation, Customs and Excise, Passports Organisation and Railways.

### *Using Non-governmental Sources*

Partnerships and outsourcing have been the hallmark of successful IT applications at all levels of government. Maharashtra franchised the entire operation of computerising the registration of documents, and Andhra Pradesh expanded the e-Seva operation with a private provider offering to invest in equipment, infrastructure, maintenance and technical staff in return for assured receipt of user charges paid by the public. Municipal corporations like Ludhiana and Mirzapur (Uttar Pradesh) have signed contracts with private agencies to computerise all records on a build, operate and transfer (BOT) basis.

**_Box 8.1_ ICT Projects Showcased by Central Government**

1 and 2. Andhra Pradesh e-Seva and CARD

3 WARANA Cooperative Complex in Maharashtra, the primary objective of which is to demonstrate the effective contribution of an IT infrastructure to the accelerated socio-economic development of a cluster of 70 contiguous villages around Warana in the Kolhapur and Sangli Districts.

4. SETHU, the citizen facilitation centre in district offices – an instance of public-private partnership which offers one stop counter services for all certificates and permits, public grievance redress and information relating to all administrative processes.

5. FRIENDS, a Citizen Friendly Service Centre set up by the Kerala Government providing 20 computerised counters, offering payment facilities for utility bills, basic and other taxes, traders licence fee, revenue recovery, fee for new ration card, motor vehicle tax, etc.

6. BHOOMI, Government of Karnataka is a comprehensive land records computerisation system with fully online facilities to carry out changes in land records data, based on biometrics, to ensure foolproof authentication and enforce non-repudiation. It provides the facility to scan the field mutation orders passed by revenue authorities, notices served, etc., and provides information through a touch screen kiosk.

7. Simplified and Transparent Administration of Registration (STAR) of the Government of Tamil Nadu, is a computerised service for land record transactions, certified copies, computerised registration process, property valuation, registration of marriages/societies, firms, chits, etc. with archival facilities for scanning, storage and retrieval of records.

8. GYANDOOT – Project of the Government of Madhya Pradesh in Dhar district – is a computer network connecting rural cyber centres. It is operated by trained unemployed youth. It caters to the people's everyday needs by providing information and transacting services relating to commodity marketing information system, Income Certificate, Domicile Certificate, Caste Certificate, landholder's passbook of land rights and loans, rural Hindi e-mail, public grievance redress, forms for various government schemes, list of families below poverty line, *Employment News*, rural matrimonial (Vivah Sambandh), rural market (Gaon ka Bazaar), rural newspapers, Driving Licence.

These arrangements help cash-strapped states avoid the need for initial large outlays for IT applications with commercial potential. Vishakapatnam (Andhra Pradesh) has expanded its online system of assessment and collection of property taxes by enabling customers to access bank branches, which in turn operate on the municipal tax base. With transparent systems of inviting and evaluating bids, many small companies have been able to enter the field. Many departments and some states have engaged reputable multinational and Indian companies to help in formulating the blueprint for ICT and then in selecting the providers for individual applications.

## 8.2 E-governance and Citizen Concerns

While corruption has not been stated to be the main focus of e-governance, it is expected that transparency, easy access to information on government procedures and virtual processes will reduce the scope for corruption, especially in areas like hospitals, civil supplies, urban development, electricity and water supplies. The reasons for reduction in corruption at the level of the middleman can be attributed to the large-scale computerisation of services, reforms initiated by the vigilance departments and the rise in awareness among consumers.

Pioneering initiatives in transparency through ICT tools include the 'Computerised check posts' project for sales tax in Gujarat and other states and the Karnataka civil society campaign to publish and debate financial analyses of local bodies. Another visible application has been in the field of procurement, as bids and tenders for public works are widely perceived to be the fountainhead of corruption in local government. Saukaryam in Vishakapatnam has addressed this issue by an e-enabled disclosure process of publishing all financial transactions – bidding and auctions, decisions, tenders, procurement, etc. – through the internet so that they are in the public domain. Electronic procurement has advanced considerably in states like Andhra Pradesh, Delhi, Tamil Nadu and Karnataka, reducing delays and increasing transparency.

One undisputed impact of the ICT revolution is the widening of the space for participation and contestation. Gyandoot (Madhya Pradesh) has piloted e-extension services of the central Ministry of Agriculture and similar local initiatives provide a facility for citizens to lodge their grievances. It is evident that internet-based advocacy campaigns such as the campaign by a consortium of NGOs on probity in the electoral processes and the devolution of power to PR bodies have the potential to get governments to respond.

NGOs and research agencies are involved in extending services and information to people using ICT. Instances are the Swaminathan Foundation in Pondicherry, the Dhan Foundation's information centres in Tamil Nadu and the Azim Premji Foundation and literacy project in Karnataka. The corporate sector, including the National Association of Manufacturers of Computers and Software Providers, is closely associated with government initiatives at the policy-making and operational level. Many states and central ministries are outsourcing some or all activities in ICT enterprises like CARD and SETU in order that the operations are sustained in either the build, operate, lease and transfer (BOLT) or the BOT mode.

**Box 8.2 IT and Equity**

**Many initiatives that give information about policies and programmes and deliver government documents are attempts at equity and at extending entitlements to rural populations. In many cases, such as in the RASI Maiyams of Kanchipuram district (Tamil Nadu) and the e-Seva initiative in West Godavari district (Andhra Pradesh), micro-enterprise models for promoting employment through kiosks have focused on socially disadvantaged populations. The Andhra Pradesh project brings together women SHGs in villages under various central and state development and welfare schemes and helps them with financing and self-help initiatives. With the help of technology, the Government of Haryana is able to deliver to its citizens a social security system which is more transparent. The partnership between the Government of Karnataka and the Azim Premji Foundation to establish and run community learning centres in schools in rural areas, especially in certain backward districts, aims at equipping rural schools with state of the art learning resources driven by IT. Use of popular interactive modes like cable TV, publication of school examination results and making available downloadable government forms have driven wider use of government websites by users.**

Thee are several examples of units like kiosks or information counters offer different types of content and revenue based or free services (for e-govemance and other focus areas) over a network to individuals, groups and communities, and help to break the digital divide. They include citizen or farmer services and e-choupal (markets) through rural kiosks in Dhar and other districts, Mahiti Shakti (women's power) Panchmahal, Gujarat and various community information centres. The central initiative of Vidya Vahini connects 5,000 high schools in seven districts. It provides real time audio and video interactivity – lectures can be conducted in 5,000 schools simultaneously.

## 8.3 E-governance in States

Examples from states can be seen in the previous and present sections. Some state governments have built a few applications on an extensive scale covering the delivery of specific services to a large proportion of the population, such as online registration of property transactions or land records and driving licences, or a large number of departments in areas like HRM and Treasury. With a widely dispersed network of public offices for service delivery and administration, state governments have concentrated from the beginning on wide area networks and connectivity.

Procedural and regulatory reforms and systematic data input have preceded many flagship applications like CARD in Andhra Pradesh. Land registration offices throughout Andhra Pradesh and Maharashtra operate computerised counters to help citizens to complete registration requirements within one hour instead of the several days which were needed under the manual system. The Vijayawada system in Andhra Pradesh (a finalist in the Stockholm Challenge competition) was able to deliver municipal services in several kiosks because of the re-engineering of back-end processes and linking the kiosks to the wide area network.

The health sector is distinguished by the example of tele-medicine in Tamil Nadu, Andhra Pradesh and Maharashtra, which can provide remote consultation and emergency facilities as well as treatment online. Andhra Pradesh provides an example of enabling auxiliary nurse midwives to use hand-held computers to eliminate redundant paperwork and data entry, freeing time to deliver health care to poor people.

State governments have used IT for services that increase the productivity and income of communities as in Warana, Maharashtra and the Gujarat Agriculture Extension Project, so that producers receive better returns for their produce. After a big earthquake, Maharashtra became the first state in the country to implement a comprehensive disaster management plan (DMP), complete with a state-of-art satellite-linked computer network connecting various civic bodies, offices of collectors and sub-districts in the state. The revolutionary increase in the supply of milk of improved quality in the co-operative sector, starting with Gujarat, is partly the result of computerised processes of testing and buying milk at decentralised locations. The interaction with the milk producers has extended to veterinary and other services, thus impacting on directly on poverty.

Eighteen languages are recognised as official languages under the Indian Constitution. To enable people to access these new technologies, software has been developed that transforms text – and will soon convert speech – automatically from one language to another, thus benefiting blind people as well. All websites in states like Tamil Nadu operate on the bilingual mode.

Gujarat was in the limelight when it introduced the smart card-based driving licence project. Each of the Regional Transport Offices (RTOs) of Gujarat was equipped with state-of-the-art enrolment and issuance centres. The government has also implemented a state-wide WAN (Wide Area Network) project that connects its various office complexes and corporations and supports services like voice, data and video traffic. Similarly, Tamil Nadu Virtual Private Network (TNVPN) which is based on a public-private partnership deal, will link all government departments to provide voice, data and video connectivity and improve the delivery of services to citizens.

With the introduction of the RD Net project, the Government of Kerala has connected all the 152 block offices in the state – providing for uninterrupted co-ordination of their activities. More importantly, it set up 'Information Kerala Mission' with a view to transforming local bodies into genuine institutions of self-government. It aims to enable ordinary citizens to access relevant information in the Malayalam language over the internet. The Office of Controller of Entrance Examinations has been automated to bring about transparency in allocation of colleges to successful students.

Indian professionals have developed methods for making people literate using IT, which skips the sequence of learning and by which almost 40,000 persons who were totally illiterate have been brought to a level that they can now read newspapers on their own. The path-breaking Akshaya project in Kerala (much lauded in international competitions) is aimed at entrepreneurship development and mass employment generation in the IT sector in the state, which is in turn linked to a mass e-literacy programme.

Since about 70 per cent of the population lives in rural areas, rural kiosks are increasingly serving as multi-function centres delivering services and information that cuts across departmental boundaries. Government has realised that these kiosks, operated by local youth or NGOs, are the only way a sufficient number of people can come to these centres and use the services to make the whole operation viable.

Significant efforts have been made in applying ICT in the areas of financial management and personnel policies. The online data capture and central consolidation of all of Karnataka's financial transactions is being networked through a system called 'Khazane', or Treasury and it is proving to be a model for other states. The Interactive Voice Response System provides the latest information on the status of pending bills to drawing officers and the public. Payroll has been computerised in many states. Dynamic computerised databases on government personnel are being installed in Uttar Pradesh, Andhra Pradesh and Punjab. IT-based secretarial reforms have been described elsewhere.

Revenue collection has increased significantly due to the reduction of leakage, more automated processes, scope for more effective monitoring and greater citizen compliance and satisfaction. By just computerising water/sewerage and house tax billing, payments and receipts, the Ludhiana Municipal Corporation in Punjab state discovered arrears worth Rs. 400 million. Revenue can be augmented by many municipal corporations by computerising and constantly updating records of property tax, municipal assets, water charges, trade licences, rental properties and accounts.

Many state governments are setting up a 'e-government gateway' that will enable various service providers to interact with backend databases and applications of various departments to provide cost-effective services to citizens and businesses. City-wide information systems are operational in several large cities structured often on city level partnerships with business. The Karnataka government will soon

**Box 8.3 Selected E-governance Initiatives in Andhra Pradesh**

CARD – This project was introduced to speed up the process of registering deeds from a couple of weeks to less than an hour. By September 2000, the CARD process had registered around 1.1 million documents in its first 22 months of operation. There are 214 computerised centres in Andhra Pradesh, and the project has been rightly acclaimed by independent examiners as one of the most effective examples of e-governance in India.

APSWAN – This project is a dedicated fibre optic network for voice, data and video communication that connects the Government in Hyderabad with 23 district headquarters and the cities of Vijayawada and Tirupati.

E-Seva – The E-Seva project provides an integrated single window service with private sector involvement for 43 separate government services, from paying utility bills and taxes, to obtaining birth certificates, to purchasing train tickets, at over 27 service centres throughout Hyderabad and surrounding municipalities. Over 800,000 citizens have been served since the service was initiated in August 2001. Currently, well over half a million transactions take place each month, with an average service time of two minutes off-peak and 15 minutes at peak time. Plans are currently underway to extend the service to 229 more sites in all 117 municipalities. A parallel initiative that seeks to provide instant access to over 60 services in rural areas, called the On-line Transaction Processing (OLTP) programme, is currently being piloted in two districts.

APDMS – This project is a geographically based information system that has created base maps of all of the 1,122 mandals and constituent revenue villages and habitations. Applications can superimpose thematic data on the road network, community infrastructure, basic demographic data, soil and geomorphological data. These data are available on the internet and support research, analysis, project design and monitoring.

SKIMS – This project was initiated with the objective of improving the management of information and knowledge within the Secretariat. The goal is to increase employee productivity and satisfaction, streamline and speed up the circulation of files and other documents, and facilitate the placement of government information on the internet for public access.

MPHS – The MPHS has created a computerised database of socio-economic information on 76.7 million citizens. It is comprised of over 100 difficult fields of information in areas ranging from basic social and demographic data to legal records and access to the public distribution. It covers all 1,122 mandals or sub-districts throughout the state.

be launching a single point delivery mechanism for e-governance called Bangalore One. Box 8.3 gives details of some of the significant applications in Andhra Pradesh.

## 8.4 The Way Ahead

Despite the interest shown by all states, only few states are assessed as e-ready and others are busy catching up with successful modes and articulating strategies with the help of central government. The lagging states are focusing on the following elements of e-governance strategy:

- Articulating a vision and strategy in the context of governance reform with a dedicated department and co-ordination mechanisms within government;
- Developing a road map of the major projects that would be undertaken over a three-year time frame with clear idea of costs and benefits;
- Developing best practices and guidelines;
- Taking responsibility for applications that cut across departments and developing flagship applications like *Bhoomi* and CARD;
- Creating and maintaining common infrastructure with the WAN reaching up to sub-districts;
- Greater penetration of personal computers and access to internet especially in villages;
- Building human capacity at various levels;
- Independently auditing all projects for the benefits and client feedback;
- Strengthening online procedures including e-kiosks for grievance redress and transactions;
- Raising public awareness and forming partnerships with private sector academic institutions The success of e-governance is not about technological marvels; rather, it is about whether and how good governance has been attained through technology. E-govemance must be backed by administrative reforms in processes, procedures, attitudes and systems of governance and continuing efforts to standardise guidelines and standards.

# 9 Administrative Reform in Indian States

Fiscal crisis generated a systemic crisis during the 1990s and has now given a huge momentum to central and state efforts for fiscal and administrative reforms. While charting the second phase of the strategy of reform and liberalisation in India, there is a consensus that many of the reforms which are required to accelerate India's growth and poverty reduction need to be implemented by the states. These include not only fiscal reforms to address resource constraints, which are increasingly circumscribing the states' developmental role, but also power sector reforms to address a fundamental source of fiscal pressure and constraint to growth, and governance reforms to make state governments smaller, more accountable and effective in the delivery of services. Donor agencies like the World Bank and Asian Development Bank are assisting reform in states through structural adjustment loans and sector level support. Financial institutions have started rating the state governments, functional agencies and cities with objective criteria for grading their access to loans and the capital market.

A number of state governments such as Andhra Pradesh, Gujarat, Madhya Pradesh and Uttar Pradesh have proceeded systematically through the formulation of vision statements or strategies based on consultation with all stakeholders and experts. Task Forces for Good Governance have been appointed in Andhra Pradesh, Orissa and Maharashtra, while Administrative Reform Commissions/Committees have been appointed in Kerala, Karnataka, Uttar Pradesh, Tamil Nadu and Maharashtra. States like Kerala, Madhya Pradesh and Karnataka have carried the exercise down to local government level and vigorously implemented committee reports and amended laws and procedures to make devolution more meaningful. The entire exercise has been characterised by transparency and widespread consultation, with striking exercises in development communication.

Some of the newly created states are as aggressive in reforms as the first generation leaders. Since its creation, the state of Chhattisgarh has achieved a target that the wage bill will not exceed 40 per cent of own source revenues and it has drastically reduced the number of departments and public undertakings. Other new states, such as Uttaranchal, are exercising similar restraint. The Department of ARPG has been documenting the initiatives of different states and the details of reforms are also available on the websites of individual states. The reforms can be considered under a number of heads.

### *Decision-making, Centralisation and Procedural Logjams*

**_Box 9.1_ Civil Service Reforms in States**

Striking examples of reform include:

- Publication of a politically owned strategy paper on good governance and civil service reform with sequenced annual plans for implementation (Andhra Pradesh, Karnataka, Orissa and Kerala).
- Organisation of a comprehensive and computerised personnel database and linking this to the computerisation of Treasury and Payroll (Uttar Pradesh, Punjab and Andhra Pradesh).
- Vesting responsibility for civil service reform and responsive administration in the General Administration or Administrative Reforms Department under the Chief Secretary (Andhra Pradesh, Karnataka, Orissa and Maharashtra).
- Zero-based functional audits of key departments (preceded by quick functional reviews) based on a inventory of schemes, identification of redundant schemes, staff and associated activities. Redundant staff are offered redeployment, voluntary retirement or in some instances face termination with benefits (Orissa, Karnataka and Maharashtra).
- Increasing resort to contract mode of appointment and lateral entry with adequate safeguards (Andhra Pradesh and Karnataka).
- Consolidating cadre rules and regulations related to civil service to pursue systematic revision with due regard to causes for service litigation and effective performance.
- Devising computerised procedures for secretariat information and monitoring file movement such as *Smartgov* (in Andhra Pradesh) and other simpler systems .

States such as Andhra Pradesh and Karnataka and some of the smaller states like Chhattisgarh and Delhi provide many instances of simplification of financial and administrative procedures, departmental autonomy for spending, personnel and approvals, delegation of powers, and specification of time limits for decisions. In Uttar Pradesh, departments are free to spend money on continuing schemes once the budget has been approved by the Governor. Departmental file movement has been computerised in a number of southern states and inter-departmental matters are dealt with quickly by empowered committees. Major exercises for the revision of manuals and secretariat procedures are under way in other states, for example revising financial authorisation powers to account for inflation and prescription of time limits for different types of cases.

### *Machinery of Government: Rationalisation of Functions and Staff*

The two major components of reform in the Indian states of Andhra Pradesh and Karnataka are: i) simplifying, redefining and rationalising government's role to focus on the most critical public goods and services; and ii) enhancing the accountability, responsiveness and transparency with which the government and its agencies perform this role. Andhra Pradesh coined the term SMART (Simple, Moral, Accountable, Responsive and Transparent) for its vision of governance.

The Modernising Government Programme strategy of Kerala contemplates an approach to development that rest on five pillars such as service delivery, decentralisation and focus on core functions of government. Karnataka has proceeded systematically to implement the report of the report of the Administrative Reforms Commission. Its legislation on freedom of information, fiscal policy and procurement are models for other states.

Many states have initiated serious exercises to merge, abolish or consolidate departments, undertake functional reviews and zero-based audit of schemes and staff. Some of them are streamlining reporting levels based on organisational charts. Orissa is a leader among Indian states on the front of privatisation of public enterprises in sectors where the public sector has proved to be inefficient and non-essential. It was the first state to privatise electric power distribution. It is also ahead of other states in terms of the number of public enterprises, which have been closed, divested or privatised followed by downsizing of the PSU workforce.

### *Box 9.2* Meritocracy in States

- Rightsizing exercises in Andhra Pradesh, Orissa, Karnataka, Punjab, Goa, Chhattisgarh and Maharashtra with a range of measures for abolition of vacant posts, freeze on posts and recruitment, phasing out work-charged staff, premature retirement, phasing out of compassionate appointments, redeployment of surplus staff, and attractive schemes for voluntary retirement;
- Departmental Recruitment Committees, on the model of GOI and Andhra Pradesh, to draw up an annual plan for filling posts with due regard to attrition, continuation of temporary and permanent posts related to Plan schemes and non-Plan activities, essentiality of posts, modes of recruitment and reservation and the shortage of staff in backward districts;
- Transfer policies based on stable tenure, transparency and consultation with employees, as in Andhra Pradesh and Karnataka;
- Merit-based recruitment for posts based on different modes of recruitment for core and non-core posts, and Collector's control over field staff (in Andhra Pradesh);
- Increasing attention to performance assessment at secretariat and field levels through steps like improved system of confidential rolls, clear links to promotion, training, continuance in service and career planning and the use of tangible performance indicators (in Andhra Pradesh);
- Efforts to streamline and reduce delays in departmental enquiries;
- Training workshops, video-conferences and other modes to improve two way communication.

### *Making Government Accountable and Responsive to Citizens and E-governance*

The elements of citizen-centred administration in states include:

- Operationalisation of laws for freedom of information;
- Formulation and credible implementation of citizen's charters;
- Speedy and effective redress of public grievances;
- Simplification of rules and regulations;
- Decentralisation and partnerships with NGOs and the private sector;

### *Box 9.3* Centre for Good Governance

A major challenge in Andhra Pradesh was to create a base within the government to help 'institutionalise' the governance reform process. This task involves conducting the requisite analytic work in support of reforms, validating the findings and monitoring their implementation. CGG was set up in January 2002 in the campus of the state HRD Institute to meet this need.

The Centre has a high-powered management board under the chairmanship of the Chief Minister and a substantial complement of professional staff to assist the Executive Director. The Centre's key priorities are to work with government departments and the general public along six major dimensions related to the SMART agenda:

1. Improving delivery of services by simplifying government;
2. Improving human resource management and ethical values in public service;
3. Developing systems for accountability, including performance indicators;
4. Making government more responsive to citizens, especially the poor, through decentralisation and participatory development;
5. Increasing transparency of administration and financial management, and;
6. Improving the performance and policy analysis capacity of government departments.

The Centre has conducted detailed studies on practical issues like the management of service litigation, streamlining disciplinary cases, working of the CARD scheme, citizen's charters and grievance redress, and has developed IT applications in areas like monitoring of government litigation and increasing the effectiveness and transparency of spending on public works. It is working closely with the state's governance and public management Unit and HRD Institute in piloting many applications for ultimate transfer to individual departments.

- Easy and widespread access to information on government schemes and procedures and computerised access of land records (such as *Bhoomi* in Karnataka);
- Similar examples of electronic governance to those described above;
- Facilitation of transactions with public agencies through computerised counter services or virtual sites (such as e-Seva in Andhra Pradesh, JAGRITI in Punjab, FRIENDS in Kerala);
- Increasing numbers of innovative city mayors and the chairpersons of rural PRI bodies;
- Opportunities for local consultation and participation in budgeting, service delivery and resource allocation (such as *Janagraha* in Bangalore or *Bhagidari* in Delhi);
- Documentation and dissemination of good practices within and across states

### *Policy Analysis*

A number of state governments have set up centres dedicated to good governance and enhancement of policy skills of officers. Maharashtra has set up a centre for good governance in its ATI. Andhra Pradesh government set up the Centre for Good Governance in 2002.

# References

Appleby, Paul (1953). *Public Administration in India: Report of a Survey*, Manager of Publications, Government of India, New Delhi.

Government of India (1962). *Committee on the Prevention of Corruption*, Ministry of Home Affairs, New Delhi.

——— (1969). *Reports of Administrative Reforms Commission on Machinery of the Government of India and Procedures of Work; Personnel Administration and State Administration*, Manager of Publications, Government of India, New Delhi.

——— (1983). *Report of Economic Reforms Commission*, Ministry of Finance, New Delhi.

——— (1997a). *Action Plan for Effective and Responsive Administration*, Department of Administrative Reforms and Public Grievances, New Delhi.

——— (1997b). *Statement of the Conference of Chief Ministers on Effective and Responsive Administration*, Department of Administrative Reforms and Public Grievances, New Delhi.

——— (1997). *Report of Fifth Central Pay Commission* (three volumes), Ministry of Finance, New Delhi.

——— (1998a). *Report of best practices in responsive and effective administration in the states*, Department of Administrative Reforms and Public Grievances, New Delhi.

——— (1998b). R*eports of Committees on Procedural Reforms in Service Litigation, Vigilance Pocedures, Recruitment Rules and Appointment of Senior Management*, Department of Administrative Reforms and Public Grievances, New Delhi

——— (1998c). *Report of the Commission on Review of Administrative Law*, Department of Administrative Reforms and Public Grievances, New Delhi.

——— (1998). *Report of Expert Group on Motivation and Performance Evaluation*, Department of Personnel and Training, New Delhi.

——— (1999). *Report of Committee on Vigilance*, Department of Administrative Reforms and Public Grievances, New Delhi.

——— (2001). *Reports of Task Forces on Vigilance, Appointment of Senior Officials Service Litigation and Financial Rules*, Department of Administrative Reforms and Public Grievances, New Delhi.

——— (2001). *Report of the Expenditure Reforms Commission*, Ministry of Finance, New Delhi.

——— (2002). *Report of Core Group of ARPG and State Governments on Administrative Reform*, Department of Administrative Reforms and Public Grievances, New Delhi .

——— (2003). *Quality Management in Government: Theory and Practice*, Department of Administrative Reforms and Public Grievances, Allied Publishing Private Ltd., New Delhi.

——— (2003). *Report of the Group Constituted to Review the System of Performance Appraisal, Promotion, Empanelment and Placement for the All India Services and Other Group A Services*, Department of Personnel and Training, New Delhi.

——— (2003). *Annual Report 2002–2003*, Department of Personnel and Training, New Delhi.

——— (2003). *Economic Survey 2002–2003*, Ministry of Finance, New Delhi.

——— (2003). *Annual Report, 2002–2003*, Ministry of Rural Development, New Delhi.

——— (2003). *Annual Report, 2002–2003*, Ministry of Information Technology, New Delhi.

——— (2000). *Report of Task Force on Reforms in Administration*, Prime Minister's Office, New Delhi.

——— (2002). *Tenth Five Year Plan*, Planning Commission, New Delhi.

——— (2002). *Millennium Study of Public Services in India*, Public Affairs Centre, Bangalore .

Government of Andhra Pradesh (1999a). *Report of Task Force on Good Governance*, General Administration Department, Hyderabad.

——— (1999b). *Vision 2020*, Planning Department, Hyderabad.

——— (2000). *Report of the Cabinet Sub-committee on Administrative Reforms*, General Administration Department, Hyderabad.

Government of Karnataka (200la). *Interim Report of the Administrative Reforms Commission*, Department of Administrative Reforms, Bangalore.

——— (2001b). *Final Report of the Administrative Reforms Commission*, Department of Administrative Reforms, Bangalore.

Government of Kerala (200la). *Report of the Committee on Administrative Reforms*, General Administration Department, Thiruvananthapuram.

——— (2001b). *White Paper on State Finances*, Finance Department. Thiruvananthapuram.

Government of Maharashtra (2001). *Report of the Committee on Good Governance*, General Administration Department, Mumbai.

——— (2003). *Report of the Committee on Administrative Reforms*, General Administration Department, Mumbai, India.

Government of Orissa (2002). *White Paper on Public Expenditure Management and Administrative Reform*, Finance Department, Bhubaneshwar.

Government of Tamil Nadu (1997). *Report of the High Level Committee on Administrative Reforms and Prevention of Corruption*, Department of Personnel & AR, Chennai.

Swami Publications (2001). *Fundamental Rules and Central Civil Services (Pension) Rules of Government of India*, Swami Publications, New Delhi.

Maheshwari, S.R. (1999). *Machinery of Government in India*, Department of Administrative Reforms and Public Grievances, New Delhi.

——— (2000). *State Governments in India*, Macmillan India Ltd., New Delhi.

Saxena, Naresh (2002). *Rationalization of Manpower in India*, Institute of Applied Manpower Research, New Delhi.

Varma, Arvind (2002). *Streamlining Departmental Inquiries*, Institute of Applied Manpower Research, New Delhi.

Sundaram, Pachampet (1998). *Strategy for Capacity Building of Urban Government Institutions in India*, National Institute of Urban Affairs, New Delhi.

World Bank (1999). *Uttar Pradesh Fiscal and Public Enterprise Reform Project*, World Bank, Washington, DC.

——— (2001a). *Karnataka Economic Restructuring Project*, World Bank, Washington, DC.

——— (2001b). *Andhra Pradesh Economic Reform Loan*, World Bank, New Delhi.

——— (2003). *India: Sustaining Reform and Reducing Poverty*, World Bank, New Delhi.

Websites of central and state government departments of India. The single entry point for accessing the web sites of the central ministries/departments and state governments is: *http://goidirectory.nic.in*